Your Guide to Great Rubber Stamping

Millions of people are rubber stamping and so many more would love to try it. While we love the wonderful cards and other projects we see in stamp stores, we've been confused! It seems like you need a class to do every project. That sounds like fun, but we often don't have the time. So we set out to uncover the basics, the tips, the hints and techniques about this craft. Our goal was to put all that information into one book with tons of wonderful projects so that we would be able to pick up a stamp (any stamp) and immediately know lots of ways to use it. We wanted to understand rubber stamping so we could be successful, too.

published by:

HOT OFF THE PRESS INC.

©2000 by **HOT OFF THE PRESS** INC. All rights reserved. No part of this publication may be reproduced or utilized in any form or by any means, including photocopying, without permission in writing from the publisher. Printed in the United States of America.

The information in this book is presented in good faith; however, no warranty is given nor are results guaranteed. Hot Off The Press, Inc. disclaims any liability for untoward results.

The designs in this book are protected by copyright; however, you may make the designs for your personal use or to sell for pin money. This use has been surpassed when the designs are made by employees or sold through commercial outlets. Not for commercial reproduction.

Warning: Extreme care must be exercised whenever using an embossing heat tool, as burns may result. Never leave a child unattended with an embossing heat tool.

Hot Off The Press wants to be kind to the environment. Whenever possible we follow the 3 R's—reduce, reuse and recycle. We use soy and UV inks that greatly reduce the release of volatile organic solvents.

For a color catalog of nearly 750 products, send $2.00 to:

HOT OFF THE PRESS INC.
1250 N.W. Third, Dept. B
Canby, Oregon 97013
phone (503) 266-9102
fax (503) 266-8749
http://www.paperpizazz.com

We contacted Rubber Stampede, one of the best in the business. They accepted the mission of this book with enthusiasm. Led by Lynn Damelio and her staff, they patiently taught us rubber stamping and produced the wonderful projects in this book.

It has taken eight months of glorious stamping, careful photography and detailed editing. We are thrilled with the variety and excellence of Rubber Stampede's designs as well as their fine products. We appreciate their dedication to the production of this book. We extend a very warm "thank you" to each of the wonderfully talented employees who created these projects. In alphabetical order, they are:

- Clara Arriaga
- Lynn Damelio
- Andi Errington
- Chris Errington
- Susana Espinoza
- Trish Heaney
- Billy Lambrinides
- Mark Menary
- Erin Shetterly
- Grace Taormina

RUBBER STAMPEDE, INC.

967 Stanford Avenue
Oakland, CA 94608

Hot Off The Press Production Credits...

President: Paulette Jarvey
Project Editor: Kris Andrews
Editor: Lynda Hill
Graphic Designer: Jacie Pete
Photographer: John McNally
Digital Imagers: Victoria Gleason, Larry Seith

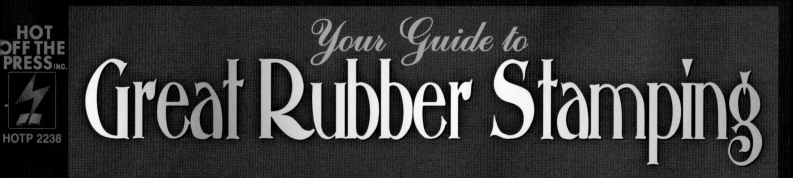

Your Guide to
Great Rubber Stamping

HOT OFF THE PRESS INC.

HOTP 2238

Table of Contents

Tools & Supplies

Welcome to rubber stamping! This is actually an age-old craft that has been well tested over time. However, new looks, new stamps and new products are always coming on the market. It's a great way to express your creativity. We begin by introducing the tried and true tools to ensure your stamping success!

Rubber stamping is a craft that requires few tools. All you really need is a stamp, ink and a surface! But there are many kinds of stamps, inks and surfaces out there—your choices are shown in the following pages.

Although paper is the most popular surface to stamp upon, it is not the only one. What other types of surfaces are able to be stamped, and which offer the greatest results? This chapter sorts through and groups them to help you make sense out of all the choices.

In addition to the basic necessities of rubber stamping, there are other tools and supplies that are fun to have. Patterned scissors create great paper edges and can even be used to help sponge a border onto your project (more about that in the next chapter!). Brayers help create a patterned background of color (see page 17) and foam or sea sponges can offer a wide range of textures. Foam mounting tape can provide depth, while a bone folder ensures a smooth contour for your paper projects (see page 19).

Let's not forget about color choices, either! Besides simply using markers to color your stamped images, there are also watercolors, colored pencils, stamping and acrylic paints and colored embossing inks or powders. Each of which add beautiful, lustrous or textured color to your project (see pages 20 and 21).

While this chapter gives you a resource for lots of tools and supplies, remember, all you need to begin is a stamp, ink and a surface. Let's go!

This chapter's background paper is from Paper Pizazz™ Handmade Papers.

Rubber Stamps come in thousands of designs and enable you to create any style or express any emotion for every occasion.

Wood handled rubber stamps are the most popular and widely available stamps on the market today. These stamps consist of a rubber die that has been adhered to a foam cushion then mounted on a wood block.

Foam handled rubber stamps are mounted onto a thick, dense piece of foam. These stamps are usually sold in kit form and cost less than wood handled stamps.

Decorative foam stamps are cut from dense foam and mounted onto a thicker foam handle. They are very economical and can be made into much larger images than rubber die stamps. They are extremely pliable making stamping on curved surfaces a breeze.

Roller stamps consist of a rubber die strip with several designs on it. It's mounted on a plastic roller so that, when rolled across a stamping surface, a continuous series of images is printed. They are perfect for creating borders or strips of images (see pages 114-119).

Stamp Pads & Inks

Stamp Pads & Inks come in many shapes and sizes. They are usually made of either felt or foam and are housed in a plastic case. Generally, the surface of the pad is raised to ensure proper ink distribution to any size stamp.

Both felt and foam stamp pads are available un-inked, with a variety of inks sold separately. The ink you choose will largely depend on the surface and end use of your project.

Dye-based ink pads are water based and quick drying. They are available in a rainbow of colors on a wide range of pad sizes. Dye-based inked images look crisper and brighter when stamped on white gloss-coated papers and appear more opaque when stamped on uncoated paper stock. Because they're water-based, they may bleed or blur on very absorbent papers such as tissue or construction paper. They're not colorfast and will fade in time.

Pigment ink pads are thick, opaque and slow drying. Usually, they are sold on foam pads in a wide range of colors including metallics. Pigment inks stamp well on all types of paper; the thick consistency stamps rich color on uncoated colored paper stock. Because of its consistency, it will only dry on coated paper when embossed and provides beautifully vibrant colors to this surface. Pigment inks are fade resistant and suitable for archival applications.

Crafter's or Fabric ink is a multipurpose ink great for fabric, paper, wood and metal. These inks are available in water-based and solvent-based formulas in several different colors. Most brands require heat to permanently set them when used on fabrics (follow the manufacturer's instructions when heat setting).

Washable ink pads are water-based which makes them easier to wash from some surfaces. Some colors, though, especially those containing red dye are much more stubborn than others. It's advised to supervise children when they are using inks.

Permanent-ink pads are also available in both water-based and solvent-based formulas. These inks can be very toxic so it's important to follow the manufacturer's instructions carefully.

Waterproof ink pads are specially formulated for use with watercolors. This special formula allows you to apply watercolor paint or ink to your stamped images without any smearing or bleeding. Waterproof ink is also available in a wide range of colors.

Embossing ink pads are glycerin-based and usually clear or slightly tinted. These inks work well on both felt and foam pads. They are designed to be slow drying so that colored and metallic embossing powders can properly adhere to the stamped image. They stamp well on all types of papers and can also be used on wood, metal and some fabrics.

Rainbow stamp pads consist of individual blocks of inked felt or foam placed side-by-side in a box to create a multi-colored stamp pad. They usually consist of three or more colors and generally contain dye-based or pigment inks.

Re-inkers are small bottles of ink available in several types of inks to add to dry ink pads or to ink an uninked pad.

Stamp Care

With all these ink names like "dye-based" and "water proof", you may be concerned about the life and cleanability of your rubber stamps. But don't worry! There are many stamp cleaners specially formulated to clean inks from the rubber die without harming it. Be sure to read and follow the manufacturer's directions for using the cleanser. Baby wipes (without alcohol) and diluted window cleaner (without ammonia) also work well to clean stamp dies.

Never immerse rubber stamps in water. To clean it, stamp it on a paper towel pre-moistened with cleaner, then on a dry paper towel until there is no trace of ink. Use an old toothbrush to clean ink from any stamp crevices. Dry your stamps well after cleaning and store them lying flat, image side down, and out of the sunlight.

Paint

offers rich and vibrant colors for your stamping art done on a variety of project surfaces. Paint offers a different texture of color than ink and adheres well to wood and fabrics. The type of paint you choose depends on the stamp you use and the surface you stamp.

Stamping paints were specially developed for use with decorative foam stamps. They're water-based and stamp extremely well on fabric, paper, walls, and wood. Stamping paints have a longer "open" drying time than ordinary acrylic paints. This extra time allows you to apply several colors to the stamp to create multi-colored images. These paints are available in an assortment of colors as well as metallics. The colors blend beautifully and clean up quickly with water.

Acrylic paints dry faster than stamping paints, and can be used for many of the same applications. They provide a nice base coat when painted on wood projects and can be stamped on fabric when mixed with a textile medium. Acrylic paints come in a wide variety of colors that blend well. They also clean up with water.

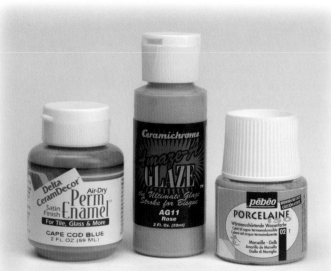

Ceramic and glass paints and glazes can require firing in a kiln, baking in an oven, or being left to air dry. Consider the intended use of the project before choosing paints and glazes. Although all will leave a permanent finish, not all are dishwasher safe or safe for use with food. Read all of the manufacturer's directions before beginning your project.

Stamping Surfaces

include just about any surface big enough to accommodate the stamp design. If you can imagine it, you can stamp on it!

Paper is by far the most popular surface used among stampers. There is a huge variety of different and unusual papers to choose from including coated, uncoated, vellum, handmade, kraft, corrugated, tissue and mulberry papers. These papers can be found in art supply, stationery, rubber stamp, and craft stores.

Uncoated papers that are very absorbent, such as construction or tissue paper, accept inks and colored markers quite readily. However, their high degree of absorbency prevents color from being richly defined. Therefore, use pigment inks which are thicker for colors that will remain vibrant even on uncoated papers.

Coated papers have a sheen or gloss which allows little or no absorbency. This creates rich and vibrant color when stamped with dye-based inks and water-based color markers—though they will smear if not allowed to dry completely. Pigment inks, however, will only dry on coated papers if embossed.

Wood is a very stampable surface both finished and unfinished. Wood can be stamped with fabric inks, crafter's inks, pigment inks, embossing inks and stamping paints. Images can be colored in with diluted stamping or acrylic paints, textile markers, watercolors or color pencils. Wood can also be embossed, just be careful not to over heat it. Water-based glazes and sealers can be used to finish the surface of the wood after stamping, if desired.

Walls of all textures can be stamped. The smoother the surface, the cleaner and clearer the image will appear. The rougher the surface, such as stucco, the more worn the image will appear.

Rubber stamps work well on walls using fabric or crafter's inks but decorative foam stamps and stamping paints will produce the best results. The large, broad surface and soft pliability of decorative foam stamps make them easier to handle than rubber stamps. Borders are the easiest wall stamping projects to begin with.

Leather can be stamped using fabric, crafter's, pigment, and dye-based inks as well as stamping paints. Smooth leather can be easily embossed, but be careful not to over heat and damage the surface. There are several leather kits available at craft stores and leather yardage is sold at some fabric stores.

Fabric projects are a favorite of stampers! Smoother fabrics such as sheeting, muslin and cotton jersey (T-shirts) stamp more successfully than others. More textured, nappy or fuzzy fabrics (such as velvet) can produce dramatic results as is shown on page 39. Practice on a scrap to prevent costly mistakes. Always wash and iron fabric before stamping and lay it out on a flat surface with scrap paper or cardboard between the layers and underneath the fabric to prevent color bleed through.

Use fabric inks, crafter's inks or stamping paints for best results. Textile or fabric markers work well to color images as do watered down stamping paints, and translucent fabric paints.

"forget me not" pillow on page 56, lamb pillow on page 60, bunny pillow on page 77

Polymer clay is sold under brand names such as Sculpey® and Fimo®. It's a soft and moldable clay that's very easy to stamp on using pigment and permanent inks or acrylic paints. Polymer clay can also be stamped without using ink or paint leaving an imprint of the image.

After stamping, the clay is baked in the oven and becomes a hard, durable plastic. Be sure to read all of the manufacturer's instructions.

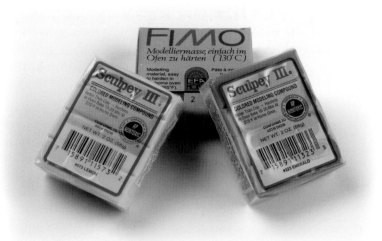

turnip plate on page 64

Ceramic is a fun surface to stamp if you have access to a ceramic studio or kiln. The colors will be most vivid stamped on unfinished (bisqueware) ceramic because the glaze adheres very well to its extremely rough surface. Stamping a single coat of ceramic glaze will give you a very light image. If a deeper color is desired, use a paintbrush to paint over the stamped image with another coat of each glaze color before firing. Both rubber and decorative foam stamps will give you great results.

Glass and porcelain can be stamped on using gloss enamel inks and acrylic enamel paints that have been specially formulated for stamping on glass and porcelain. Stamping paints can also be used if the piece is going to serve as a decorative piece only. Decorative foam stamps will give the best results because of their pliability. Glass can also be decoupaged from the back using papers stamped with rubber and decorative foam stamp images. This technique can be used for decorative purposes only (see the birthday plate project on page 81).

Follow the manufacturer's instructions to prepare the glass for painting. Be careful when stamping on glass because it's slick and the stamps are more likely to slide. If this happens, wipe the glass immediately with a damp paper towel to remove the ink, dry well and try again.

Stamping Tools

such as these shown here will make the mechanics of stamping a bit easier. The real necessities of rubber stamping such as stamps, inks and papers—are few. That's the wonderful part about stamping! As you expand your tool box beyond the basics, you may want to include some of these.

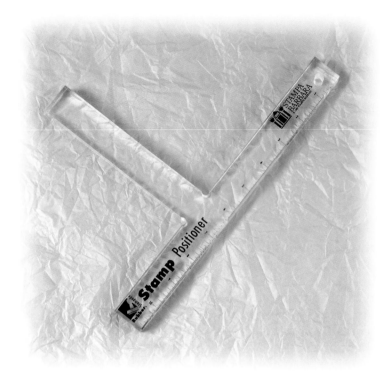

A stamp positioner is a clear acrylic tool used to place your stamped images exactly where you want them on your project. Simply place a piece of tracing paper into the right-angle corner of the tool then ink and stamp the image, also aligning the stamp in the right-angle corner. The resulting image is then used as a template. Place the template on the paper exactly where you want it, position the tool as it was for the template stamp, remove the template then ink and stamp the project surface aligning the stamp in the right-angle corner. The final image will be exactly where you had placed its template.

The stamp positioning tool is also very helpful when aligning border stamps in a straight line or to guide a roller stamp along a straight path.

A stylus is used to score cardstock before folding it. The scored line makes the fold less bulky and smoother. It's a great tool when making cards from cardstock. Page 41 gives specific instructions for doing this.

An embossing heat tool is a must if you'll be doing a lot of embossing. It's used to quickly melt embossing powders by emitting intense heat without blowing air. An embossing tool is the easiest and by far the absolutely safest way to emboss.

Alternatives are to use a hot plate, toaster or an iron. Using these, though, is hazardous. You risk personal injury or accidental damage to the paper you're embossing because the heat from these sources is harder to control. Page 28 talks more about how to use a heat tool safely.

Foam Sponges are used to apply inks and paints to rubber and decorative foam stamps. They can also be used to create a range of looks from soft, feathered backgrounds to bold blocks of color depending on the amount of pressure, ink or paint applied. These sponges are available at art and craft stores. You can also find them sold as cosmetic sponges in drug stores.

Sea Sponges are most commonly used to create backgrounds or to fill a large shape with color. Because they are nature-made, no two sea sponges are alike, and neither will be the pattern they imprint.

A brayer is used to roll color or pattern onto your background paper. You can apply patterns of color to the brayer with markers or by rolling it onto an ink pad. All types of ink will work with the exception of permanent inks. They are not recommended as they will discolor the rubber. Pages 30 and 31 show techniques for using a brayer.

Scissors and an X-acto® knife are essential tools when it comes to making rubber stamp projects. One might prefer one over the other depending on the project. The best way to cut a straight line is by using an X-acto® knife guided along the straight edge of a metal ruler. A self-healing cutting mat or scrap of cardboard is necessary to protect your work surface.

Patterned scissors are available in lots of designs and are a fun way to add interest to your paper projects. To cut uninterrupted patterns, carefully realign the blade after each cut.

Glues, Tapes and Adhesives are a must when assembling projects. Glue pens are handy for adding glitter. They can also be used to adhere thin sheets of paper together when layering and collaging. Glue sticks, glue guns, and tacky glues are perfect for heavier papers and projects. They are great for adhering charms, ribbons, buttons and other embellishments to finished projects. Remember to use acid-free, archival quality glue for scrapbook album page designs, or keepsake projects. The acidic content of some glues can make papers and photos yellow, fade or turn brittle over time.

Double stick tape can be used instead of glue on some paper projects. Masking and artist's tape is often used to create stripes or to protect what you don't want stamped or painted.

A bone folder is used for scoring and creating sharp creases in paper without tearing it. The long flat edge can also be used as a burnisher.

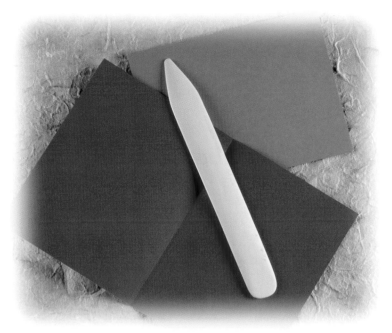

A metal ruler that is slightly raised with a cork bottom is the straight edge of choice. It can be used with an X-acto® knife to cut straight lines or with a bone folder or stylus to score straight folds. It won't allow ink to run under it and smear when drawing borders with a marker.

Foam mounting tape can be used to attach items so they rest above the background paper to create dimension. It's easy to use because you can cut the tape to the exact size needed for your project.

Foam mounting dots are small, round pieces of foam with sticky tape on both sides. They're used in the same manner as foam tape. The circular shape comes in handy for some projects.

love card on page 89

Coloring Tools such as pens, pencils and markers offer a way to make each stamped image unique. Narrow tips help color even the smallest stamp design.

Brush markers are used to color stamped images or to apply color directly to the rubber stamp. Use them for both single colored and blended effects. Brush markers are available in a rainbow of colors and many tip sizes. They contain water-based inks that clean up easily and stamp well on all papers. A blender pen can help when blending one color into the next.

Color pencils are good for coloring images when you're trying to achieve a soft, romantic look. They compliment floral imagery well and can be used on many kinds of paper but not on gloss-coated papers.

Watercolors are available in pencils, cakes and tubes. To use, mix them with water. When using watercolors, be sure to stamp your image with waterproof ink or pigment ink that has been embossed, other inks will bleed and run when the water is added. Page 26 and 27 gives more tips for using watercolors.

Fabric markers (also known as textile markers) contain permanent-ink. They work best to color in stamped images on fabric. They can also be used to color in stamped images on wood and other surfaces that normally take permanent-ink.

Embossing powders are available in a multitude of colors including metallics. They must be used with embossing or pigment inks. When heated (see page 28) the stamped image will melt and rise to a lustrous finish. It will become the color of the embossing powder or, if you're using clear powder, it will become the color of the ink.

Embossing pens come in many exciting colors and consist of a slow drying ink that can be embossed with clear powder. A colorless embossing pen can be used with colored embossing powders. They are great for embossing lines, your own handwritten message or line art. Or, stamp an image in crafter's ink, color in with these pens and emboss for a multi-colored embossed look! Page 28 gives more instruction on embossing.

Stamping Techniques

This chapter shows how to put rubber stamping tools (introduced in the previous chapter) to great use—from inking the stamp, to embossing an image, to tying a shoestring bow. If a technique is used to create a project in this book, it is explained in this chapter.

Each technique is shown in step-by-step photos with easy-to-follow text guiding you through each phase. Tools such as the bone folder, brayer, heat tool and others are shown in use, too, making it easier to understand how to use each one.

Color usage, an important part of successful stamping, is talked about in the next four pages. Color blending techniques, shown on pages 26-27, illustrate how to blend two or three colors whether you use watercolors, inks or paints.

The brayer, a funny looking tool, is featured on pages 30 and 31. It can be used to create plaid or striped backgrounds as well as solid or ghosted ones. Sponges, and all they can be used for, are explored on pages 32 and 33.

Some techniques show what to do with stamped images such as the decoupage and collage techniques on pages 34 and 35. Others talk about how best to prepare a surface such as wood, ceramics or fabric (see pages 36-38) before you stamp them—and then discuss the most successful way to stamp them.

Think velvet would be impossible to stamp? See page 39—you'll be pleasantly surprised at how easy it is. Want to stamp a border around the walls of a room? Page 40 will show you exactly what to do each step of the way!

For as many stamps that are available, there are almost as many things to do with each one of them!

This chapter's background paper is from Paper Pizazz™ Handmade Papers.

Inking A Stamp

Inking A Stamp is very simple. The trick lies in knowing how much pressure to use when applying the stamp to the pad. Too much ink will cause blurred edges, too little will stamp only a partial image.

Because a felt ink pad is dense you may need to apply extra pressure as you press the stamp onto it. A foam pad is much softer so a light touch is all that's needed to load the stamp with ink.

1 **Inking with a pad:** Press the stamp onto the surface of the pad several times until the rubber die is completely inked.

2 Stamp the project surface by applying equal pressure to the entire stamp. Don't wiggle or rock the stamp or you may blur the image. Lift the stamp straight up off of the surface.

3 Another method is to pick up the ink pad and pat it directly onto the rubber die. This works well with larger stamps.

Inking with brush markers allows you to create multi-colored images by applying different colors to certain areas of your stamp (also see page 26). Use brush markers to ink any type of stamp, though this works best when using broad surface stamps.

4 Using the broad end of the brush marker, apply the ink exactly where you want it on the rubber die. Use a different brush marker for each color of the design.

5 Before stamping the image, lightly exhale hot breath (don't blow as if to dry it) on the die to re-moisten the ink, then stamp the image.

1 Stamp the outline image on the paper. Black ink looks nice as an outline color and defines image details well.

2 Use pink to color the flower blossom along the petal edges and over the black detail lines. Use green to color the leaf detail lines. Color over the green lines with a lime or light green pencil. Color the leaf tips with the lime green pencil. Color the flower bulb lines and the roots brown.

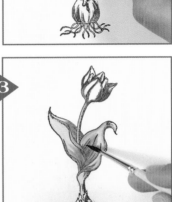

3 Dip a small liner brush into a cup of clean water. Tap the excess water from the brush and lightly brush the green pencil strokes. Sweep the brush in the same direction as the detail lines. Blend and brush the pencil color to fully shade in the leaves and stem. Blot the image with a paper towel to absorb excess water if the image is too watery. This also works if the color is too dark; blot away the excess color then dilute the color on the paper with more water. Repeat this until it's the shade you want.

4 Finally, let your artwork dry! The oval photo on page 26 shows the end result of blending colors with watercolor pencils.

Decorative foam stamps and stamping paints can create beautiful images using the color blending technique, too.

Be sure to use a separate sponge for each color to avoid mixing colors. Remember to apply the light colors before the dark colors, and to re-apply the light color along the line of two colors to achieve the gradually gradated effect.

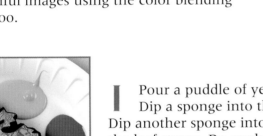

1 Pour a puddle of yellow and green paint onto a foam plate or palette. Dip a sponge into the yellow paint and dab it onto the leaf stamp center. Dip another sponge into the green paint and dab it onto the left portion of the leaf stamp. Re-apply yellow paint along the yellow and green line.

2 Pour a puddle of red paint onto the paper plate. Dip a sponge into the paint and dab it onto the right side of the image. Use the yellow sponge to re-apply yellow paint along the yellow and red line.

3 Stamp the image. Re-apply the paint for each image, taking care to use separate sponges for each color.

Embossing

Embossing creates a lustrous, raised image by bonding a slow-drying ink and embossing powder with a heat source. Paper, wood, metal, and fabric can all be embossed.

When embossing wood, take care to avoid applying heat to one area for too long as it can potentially damage the wood or finish. Be sure to use care when embossing metal as it will get very hot! Use tongs or long tweezers when handling hot metal.

Some types of glass cannot be embossed because they are not tempered to handle the necessary heat.

Embossing powders come in several colors—many of them contain glitter. For the best results use colored (opaque) powders when using clear embossing ink, and use clear (translucent) powders when using colored pigment inks.

An embossing heat tool is the easiest and safest heat source to use. It emits an intense heat without blowing air, which would scatter the embossing powder.

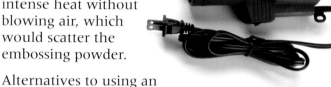

Alternatives to using an embossing tool are an iron, toaster and a hot plate. If using a toaster or hot plate, hold the paper with long tweezers and position the embossed image over the heat source until the powder melts. If using an iron, turn it to a medium-heat setting, then place the unembossed side of the paper against the iron until the powder on the other side melts.

Regardless of what type of heat source you use, take care not to burn yourself or scorch the paper. And always take precautions when children are present.

1 Stamp the image using embossing ink. Sprinkle embossing powder over the entire image. (Here, clear ink and gold embossing powder were used.)

2 Tilt the card over a piece of scrap paper then, with your finger, tap the card to remove the excess powder. The powder will cling to the stamped image. Use a small paintbrush to brush away any powder left in areas you do not want it.

3 Save the unused powder! Fold the paper to return the unused powder to its container.

4 Heat the image with an embossing heat tool until the powder melts. The heat tool should be held 1"-2" from the image and constantly moved over the image in a sweeping motion. Do not overheat the powder. The lustrous raised line of a perfectly embossed image will bubble down into liquid, spreading out over the project if overheated.

Masking

Masking an image allows you to create depth in your design as one image appears to be behind another. It also helps protect an image if a border or background color is applied to the project.

Post-it® notes or other adhesive note pads work wonderfully as stamp masks. If you need multiple masks, simply stamp the image on the top Post-it® note then remove several notes and cut them at the same time. Masking is easy, just follow these steps!

1. Stamp the flower pot bee onto your paper. Stamp it again onto a Post-it® note making sure some of the image has adhesive on the back of it.

2. Use scissors to cut out the image, cutting just inside the image line. Place the mask over the stamped flower pot bee on the paper.

3. Stamp another image overlapping the covered one so that, when you remove the mask, the second image appears to be behind the first.

A variation of masking is image isolation. Here, paint is applied only to the portion of the image you want to imprint. In this Rosebud Keepsake box, the stamp appears in its entire form only on the box sides. Stamping paint was only applied on the rose blossom portion of the stamp to stamp the box lid. Then paint was applied only to the rose leaf and stamped on each side of the blossom.

rosebud keepsake box shown at the bottom of page 94

It isn't always necessary to make image masks when building a scene. Sometimes, if the colors lend themselves to this, you can stamp over a background color. This works particularly well when the foreground color is darker than the background color. Stamping paints offer the best results because they are thicker than inks. As shown in the photo at the right, stamp or paint the light background colors, let them dry, then stamp the dark foreground colors.

cabin photo frame shown at the top of page 100

Brayering
is a quick and easy technique for applying colorful backgrounds to your stamping surface. Roll the brayer over an ink pad then roll it onto the paper to create a solid colored background. Use a rainbow ink pad to design a gradated background or use the color blending technique on page 26—you can color directly on the brayer with any marker! A brayer can also create "ghosted" images, plaids, randomly placed stamp images and more!

A successful project begins with the right tools, so remember, dye-based and water-based inks appear brighter on gloss-coated paper while pigment inks work best on uncoated papers. Waterproof ink is the best choice if you'll be coloring any images with watercolor paints or markers.

Solid backgrounds are easy to make using the brayer. Remember to stamp the foreground image first, then mask the image (see page 29).

1 Stamp the image on the paper and mask it. Roll the brayer on an ink pad using a roll-and-lift motion until the brayer roll is covered.

2 Roll the brayer over the paper. Overlap each pass until the desired color is achieved. Remove the image mask.

Plaid backgrounds are especially impressive because they look much harder to make than they really are! If desired, use markers to trace along the edge of some brayered lines or to add a thin line to the plaid after brayering.

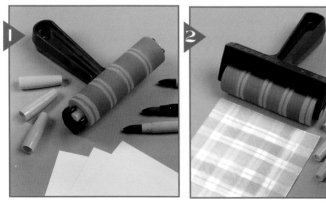

1 Use brush markers to color many bands of ink around the brayer roll. For interest, vary the distance between and the width of each band.

2 Roll the brayer over the paper in one direction to lay the stripes, then turn the paper ¼ turn and roll the brayer across the first set of stripes to lay the checks. Design diagonal plaids too!

Striped backgrounds are as simple and fun to create as plaids. Draw patterns, wavy lines or dots directly on the brayer then roll! After use, always clean your brayer with stamp cleaner.

I Use the markers to draw stripes all the way around the brayer roll. Be sure the line ends meet smoothly.

2 Breathe on the brayer roll (see page 24, step 5) to re-moisten the ink if necessary, then roll the brayer across your paper.

"Ghosted Images" make spectacular backgrounds! The air-dried embossing ink absorbs into the paper and creates a resistance to dye-based inks.

I Load the stamp with embossing ink then randomly stamp the image several times on the card—re-ink the stamp between each impression. Let the ink air dry.

2 Load the brayer with dye-based ink and roll it over the stamped card. The stamped images will begin to appear as the dye-based ink is applied.

3 Ghosted images can stand alone as shown in the step 2 photo. Or, after the ink dries, stamp over the images with a complementary or contrasting color for another look.

4 Ghosted images can also be stamped over and embossed with an image to create a very classy look!

Sponging is a fun and versatile technique used to create subtle backgrounds, borders and textures on your stamp projects.

Generally, sponging is done with foam sponges. They are available in wedge shapes, discs, or shapes like hearts or stars. Sea sponges can be used to create a wonderfully rich texture.

Sponged backgrounds are simple to do and are an easy, inexpensive way to make a textured background on your project. Still, it takes a little practice to get the proper "feel" of sponging and to achieve the look you want.

1 Pinch back the edges of a wedge sponge so that they won't leave an unwanted imprint of a solid line of color. Dab it onto a stamp pad or roll the tip of a brush marker on it to apply color.

2 Blot the sponge onto a piece of scrap paper to remove excess ink—a heavily loaded sponge leaves splotchy imprints—then dab it on the surface using a light blotting motion. Re-ink as needed.

3 Sponge each area to overlap the previously sponged areas. You may have to sponge an area several times to achieve the proper color. Use a clean sponge for each color when gradating a background. Clean the sponges for future use.

Sponged borders add a great accent. Border templates are cut with patterned scissors, offering you lots of design choices.

1 Cut the edge of a scrap piece of card stock with patterned scissors to create a template. Align this cut template ⅛" in from the card edge. Sponge color onto the edge of the card. Repeat for the other three sides.

Borders like these aren't restricted to paper projects alone. Use masking tape to protect any wood, fabric or ceramic areas you don't want inked, then apply a sponged border onto any surface you'd apply ink!

Sponged clouds use the same technique as borders (see the bottom of page 32)—cut a template and sponge around it. Cloud backgrounds are fun because they are versatile and can be used in many design or theme ideas from religious to romantic or silly to seasonal.

I Use the pattern on page 141 to cut a cloud template from cardstock. Lay it across the top of the project and sponge color around the template.

2 Pick up the template and move it down the card repeating the sponging technique until the entire background is covered. Vary the angle of the template to create a random cloud pattern.

calendar on page 97

If you're using a very light foreground color and a dark background color, consider stamping the foreground image first, then masking (see page 29) the image to sponge the background.

Sea sponges are perfect for richly textured backgrounds. They offer beautiful results on wood projects and work quite nicely on fabric, too!

I Dip the end of a slightly dampened sea sponge into a puddle of paint or dab it onto an ink pad—we used paint here. Blot any excess color onto a piece of scrap paper.

2 Dab the sea sponge onto the card until the desired look is achieved; add more paint or ink as needed.

3 Let the paint dry. Apply stamping paints to the foreground image and stamp onto the card.

Decoupage

introduces yet another means of creating with rubber stamps. Layering papers can have quite an effect on a project!

Decoupage projects have layers of cut and torn papers adhered to a surface using a decoupage medium or a clear liquid adhesive. This is another way the stamper can explore his or her creativity. As in collaging, there are no mistakes, but if you think you've made one, just cover it up with another piece of paper.

Any image can be used, and some can be embossed if you like. Use alcohol based markers, colored pencils or acrylic paints to color any images that will be decoupaged. If you use water-based markers, they'll smear when the decoupage glue is applied. Almost any surface can be decoupaged; a wood box, a cardboard or metal frame, glass, a papier mâché box, a cardboard journal and more!

1 Stamp several related images onto assorted papers with waterproof or crafter's ink. Leave some papers blank, too.

2 Cut and tear around your stamped images and plain pieces. Repeat steps 1 and 2 until you have enough papers and images to completely cover your surface.

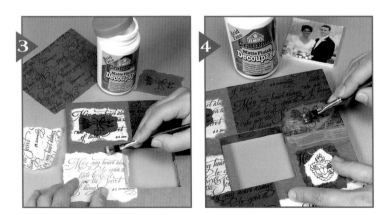

3 Overlap and adhere the pieces to your surface with decoupage glue until you are satisfied with the design.

4 The decoupage medium will act as its own sealer. However, if the project is one that will be handled often, it is a good idea to seal it with a sealer or varnish.

Collage is a wonderful way for rubber stampers to create handmade expressions of their individuality.

By adhering layers of papers, stamped images and memorabilia you can create a two-dimensional work of art that can tell a story or convey a theme.

A collage that's made up only of one stamped image adhered to a single layer of textured paper could be considered complete, while another could have several layers of torn, cut and crinkled papers along with ribbons and charms that express the designer's intent. There's no right way to construct a collage so you can't make a mistake!

Choose one or more stamps with a theme and select papers and objects that coordinate with that theme. A theme could be spring, baby, school, wedding, birthday and more. Then stamp, cut and tear your papers. Arrange the pieces until you are satisfied with the design. Glue them in place.

Adhesives are an important part of a collage. Lightweight papers require a light adhesive such as a glue stick, while heavier papers or charms require stronger glue such as a glue gun or tacky craft glue.

1 **To make the card:** Fold a 10½"x5¼" piece of cardstock in half widthwise and glue a 10½"x5¼" piece of olive paper on top (see page 41).

2 Stamp a variety of images that represent the theme of the project onto different papers. Color them as you like. Cut or tear out the images.

3 Tear pieces and strips of coordinating patterned and handmade papers to help carry the theme and for added interest. Choose charms or ribbons to include for texture.

4 Glue the pieces to the card in a free-form, random manner. Add the charms, ribbons or bows you've chosen to embellish the project.

Stamping on Wood

is quite popular among stampers. There are lots of unfinished pieces at craft stores. Finished wood pieces can include everything from your dining room chairs to bathroom shelves, and from serving trays to picture frames.

Any stamp, whether rubber die or decorative foam, works well on wood. Embossed pigment, fabric, crafter's, and permanent inks all give great results as do stamping paints. For coloring in stamped images, use textile markers, colored pencils or diluted stamping or acrylic paints.

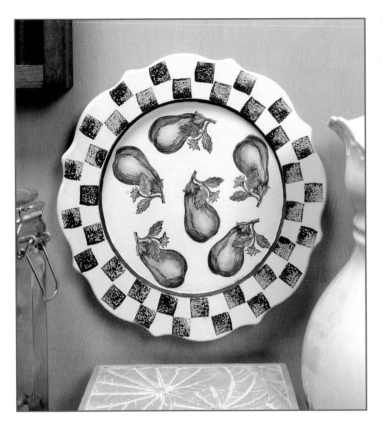

Unfinished wood projects offer the freedom of choosing whether or not the wood will be painted, and which color, or what type of sealer will be used.

All wood projects must be lightly sanded then finished with at least one coat of matte-finish acrylic wood sealer or acrylic paint (which acts as a sealer) prior to stamping. Otherwise, the ink will absorb and bleed into the wood causing the image to blur. If you're stamping with decorative foam stamps and stamping paints, sealing isn't necessary because the stamping paint won't bleed or blur (though you should still sand the rough edges).

Finished wood pieces are also fun to stamp! The finish, which can range from glossy to matte to a coat of latex paint, will dictate what stamping process gives the best result. For instance, crafter's ink adheres easily to almost any type of wood surface making it great for stamping on light-colored backgrounds, while embossed images combined with metallic ink or paint offer the most striking effect on dark-colored backgrounds.

1 Use sandpaper to lightly rub the wood until it is smooth then wipe away the dust with a soft cloth. Use a paintbrush to apply a coat of sealer or paint to the wood. Sealing it reduces paint absorption, requiring fewer coats of paint.

2 Ink the stamp and carefully stamp the image onto the wood surface—don't rock or wiggle the stamp. Lift the stamp straight up off the surface and repeat for all images. Let dry.

3 Mix one part water to one part stamping paint. Use paintbrushes to apply the colors to color in the image. Or use acrylic paint, textile markers or colored pencils.

4 If the project is intended to be handled, follow the manufacturer's instructions to apply a coat of clear sealer to the project to protect the paint.

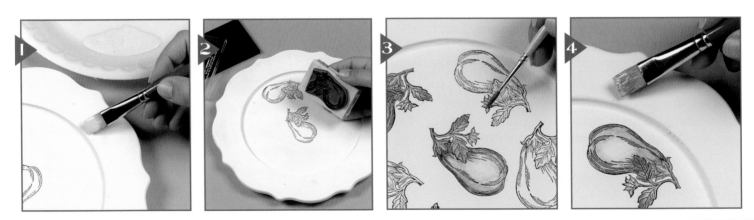

Stamping on Ceramics

creates a very distinctive look with the ease of painting or coloring in an outline. Finished ceramic projects can be used for anything from dinnerware to gift to shelf-top decorations.

There are paints and glazes on the market today that are specially formulated for stamping and painting on glazed ceramics. Some require air drying while others require being baked in your home oven. Once cured, they will be safe to use for food and microwave and dishwasher safe, too. Be sure to read the glaze manufacturer's directions before beginning.

Glazed ceramics require special care when stamping. The stamp will have a tendency to slide on the slick surface. If it slides, wipe the glaze off completely with a damp paper towel and try again. Try using a smaller rubber stamp or a small decorative foam stamp. They will be easier to handle.

Bisqueware, or unglazed ceramics, generally use ceramic glazes that will require being fired in a kiln. Decorative foam stamps impress especially nice images on bisqueware because they are soft and pliable and can easily print around curved or bumpy surfaces. Once you've completed stamping your bisque piece, it will need to be glazed and fired in a kiln. A local ceramic or pottery studio can do this for you. Pieces that have been fired in a kiln will be dish-washer safe and safe for use with food.

1 Wipe the bisqueware with a wet clean cloth to remove all flecks of dust. Shake each glaze well and pour a puddle of each color onto a foam plate.

2 Use foam sponges to apply the glaze colors to the appropriate portion of the stamp. Stamp the image onto the surface.

3 Re-apply glaze to the stamp for each impression. To achieve a deeper color, use a paintbrush to apply a second coat of glaze over the first.

4 Use paintbrushes to paint the glaze onto the background. Leave a ⅛" wide strip around each image unpainted to create a white outline.

5 Cure the piece as per the glaze manufacturer's instructions. This may require taking the piece to a professional to have it glazed and fired in a kiln.

Stamping on Fabric

creates wonderful art! It's easy to do, great to give and fun to wear or use.

Outline or broad surface rubber stamps give the best results when stamped on smoothly woven fabrics such as muslin, cotton sheeting and cotton jersey (T-shirts). Rougher fabrics such as canvas or denim look best when stamped with decorative foam stamps and stamping paints.

Fabric ink is the best ink to use for fabric stamping. Outline images can be colored in with textile markers, fabric paints or acrylic paints mixed with a textile medium.

bunny pillow shown on page 77, bee pillow shown on page 80

Fabric stamping is most successful when images with clean lines are selected. The steps below show how to use outline images to stamp your fabric. The bunny pillow in the large photo shows the results you'll see when using a broad surface decorative foam stamp. Avoid highly detailed images because the corners and crevices tend to blur; outline stamp designs and broad surface stamps are the best choices.

Always wash the fabric to remove the sizing and prevent shrinkage or dye bleeding after it's been stamped—both of which may distort the image. Because more pressure needs to be applied to a stamp when working with fabric, it's best to stand to get more leverage.

Remember that some inks and textile markers require heat setting. Be sure to read all of the manufacturer's instructions thoroughly.

It is possible to emboss on fabric with pigment ink and embossing powder, though the surface of the image may become a bit brittle.

1 Iron the fabric and lay it out on a hard, flat surface. Place a piece of cardboard under and between any fabric layers. Load the stamp with black fabric ink and stamp the image on the fabric. Repeat as desired.

2 Pour a quarter-sized puddle of each color of stamping or fabric paint onto a paper plate. Use a paintbrush to apply the color to the images. Or use textile markers to color in each image. Let dry.

Stamping on Velvet

is also referred to as heat stamping. This technique is a unique way to imprint an image onto velvet.

Stamping on velvet "brands" the image into the fabric. The heat "presses" down the velvet nap which leaves an elegant, metallic-looking sheen in the shape of the stamp image. Broad surface stamps work best for this technique, although experimenting with outline stamps could be rewarding. To achieve the cleanest impression possible, use an X-acto® knife to trim any excess rubber from around the image. It's very important to test the process on a scrap of velvet before beginning the project.

velvet photo album shown on page 62

1 Pre-heat the iron to the permanent press setting without steam. Place the stamp, rubber side up, on a hard flat surface. Lightly mist the back of the velvet with water. Lay the velvet, nap side down on the stamp.

2 Apply the hot iron to the wrong side of the velvet for 20 seconds without moving it. Make sure the steam holes do not interfere with the image.

3 Lift the iron carefully and remove the velvet. Repeat for each additional impression.

Stamping on Walls

Stamping on Walls is a unique way to decorate your home. When you finally stamp the walls in your home, you'll wonder why it took so long before you tried! Rubber stamps can be used on your walls, but the easiest way to stamp is by using decorative foam stamps and stamping paints. The soft, pliable foam makes stamping on smooth or textured walls a breeze.

Remember, a small project like stamping a wreath of flowers onto the wall or a border around a mirror is a fun way to test wall stamping before you tackle the entire room.

Wall stamping success begins with a solid plan. To help visualize the images that will border the ceiling or floor-boards, stamp several images onto scrap paper, cut them out and use masking tape to temporarily adhere each one to the wall. Experimenting with placement will show you the exact position the image looks best and give you an overall view of what your finished design will look like. Then apply the paint to the foam stamp, remove one paper pattern and stamp the image in its place.

1 Start with a clean, dry wall. Remove any pictures or wall décor that may get in the way. Stamp many images on paper, then cut around each one to use as patterns.

2 Tape the pattern pieces to the wall. Arrange the pieces until you're satisfied with the design and get ready to stamp!

3 Pour a fresh puddle of paint onto a foam plate. Make sure the stamp is clean and dry, then apply the paint to the stamp. Remove one pattern and stamp the image in its place. Repeat until all of the patterns have been removed and replaced with actual stamped images. Let dry.

4 Isolate a part of the image (as discussed on page 29) to create off-shoots on the ivy vine. Again, make sure you begin with a clean, dry stamp.

General Information

about techniques such as bow tying and card making are used throughout this book. The steps below will help you craft each project with ease!

1 **Tying a shoestring bow:** Measure the desired tail length from the ribbon end, then make a loop of the specified length. Wrap the free end loosely around the center of the bow.

2 Form a loop in the free end of the ribbon and push in through the center loop. Pull the loops in opposite directions to tighten, then adjust the loop size by pulling on the tails. Trim each tail diagonally or in an inverted "V".

3 **Matting:** Glue the stamped paper to the background paper and cut ⅛"-½" around it.

4 Repeat step 1 to double or triple mat. Tear around the mat, or use straight or patterned scissors to provide a variety of mat edges.

5 **Making a card:** Cut the cardstock to the correct height and twice the width for the finished card (for a top-folded card, cut the correct width and twice the height). On the back, measure and lightly draw a fold line along the center with the pencil.

6 Firmly hold the bone folder in place along the drawn line. Run a stylus along its edge; press firmly to score a groove in the cardstock.

7 Still holding the bone folder firmly in place, fold the cardstock on the scored line.

8 **Covering a card:** Plain cardstock can be covered with plain or textured paper. Or use Paper Pizazz™ patterned paper to create a variety of backgrounds for your stamping projects. Spray adhesives give the smoothest results. Protect your work surface with newspapers and work in a well ventilated area. Evenly spray the adhesive to cover the outside of the card.

9 Pick up the card in the center, allowing it to partially fold closed. Move it onto the paper. Use the bone folder to smooth the back card flap, then fold the paper to cover the front and smooth it.

10 **Lining a card:** Cut the liner paper slightly smaller (¹⁄₁₆") than the card flap. Spray the adhesive on the paper back and adhere to the card flap. Use the bone folder to smooth it in place.

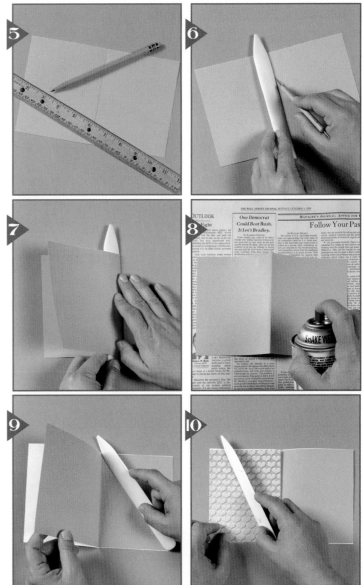

Outline Stamps

Outline stamps are the type of stamp which create an imprint of the outline of an image. They can be colored in with markers, paint or watercolors. Many outline stamps include wonderful details of an image including shadows and highlights.

Outline stamps can be inked with a pad or markers to create the impression. An ink pad is a fine way to produce an outline to be colored in such as the frog gift bag on page 45. Or, use brush markers to color directly on the stamp to achieve a multi-colored outline of the image as is shown on the peony gift box at the bottom of page 47.

The outline of an image can be embossed in gold to create a rich, gilded look like the rose stamp used on the gift wrap project on page 46. The rosebud sachet tag shows the lovely results of both embossing and coloring in an outline image.

The outline of an image can be embossed in black then colored in as shown with the balloon present paper, or embossed but left mostly uncolored as with the wacky birthday cake card (both on page 48). Page 49 shows the contrast of embossing an image and imprinting an image into polymer clay. Both are colored in but have two strikingly different looks!

Not every outline image has to be colored in to be effective in your design. The two projects on page 44 show how versatile outline stamps can be. The un-colored herb stamps provide a fresh look perfect for your favorite kitchen recipes, while the painted images on the veggie tray offer a visually appetizing way to serve healthy snacks.

Outline stamps are a wonderful tool to express your artistic creativity. They can be used in many different ways, so each outline stamp has lots of looks!

This chapter's background paper is from Paper Pizazz™ Handmade Papers.

Herb Recipe Box & Cards

herb stamps: Chives, Sweet Basil, Oregano, Garlic,
*   Rosemary*
emerald green crafter's ink
6"x4"x4" unfinished wood recipe box
3"x5" natural recipe cards
acrylic paints: ivory, black, brown
1 yard hunter green twine
½" wide flat paintbrush, toothbrush, old cloth
soft cloth, sandpaper

Prepare the wood (see page 36). Paint the box ivory; let dry. Stamp the herb images randomly on the box sides and lid. Stamp one herb image on each recipe card; bind the cards together with twine. Mix a wash of one part brown paint and two parts water then quickly wipe the wash over the wood with a cloth. Dip a damp toothbrush into black paint; pull your thumb across the bristles to spatter the box. Use the sandpaper to rub off the paint along the corners for a well-used appearance.

Veggie Tray

vegetable stamps: Small Tomato, Small
*   Eggplant, Small Artichoke*
black crafter's ink
16"x12" unfinished wood tray
acrylic paints: ivory, red, green, light green,
*   purple, yellow*
flat paintbrushes: 1" wide, ½" wide,
*   ¼" wide*
#0 liner paintbrush
pencil, eraser, ruler, scrap paper
sandpaper, soft cloth
water-based sealer

Prepare the wood (see page 36). Use the 1" wide flat brush to paint the tray ivory. To design the checkerboard, lightly draw a pencil line ½" in from the outer tray edge and continue drawing lines the length of the tray, skipping the inner tray area. Turn the tray ¼" turn and repeat the process to make checks. Use the ½" flat brush to paint every other check in the design green. Erase any visible pencil lines. Stamp several vegetable images onto scrap paper and cut them out. Place them on your project to help visualize your finished project before actually stamping it. Be sure the stamping ink is completely dry before painting the images or the ink will run. Paint the images as shown. Seal the tray.

Trout Wrapping Paper & Tag

*Trout stamp, black dye-based ink
kraft paper, wrapping paper
2¾"x3½" black cardstock
2½"x3¼" corrugated kraft paper
colored pencils: red, blue, yellow, green
2" long fishing lure, 3 gold snap swivels
natural twine, tacky glue, ¼" hole punch*

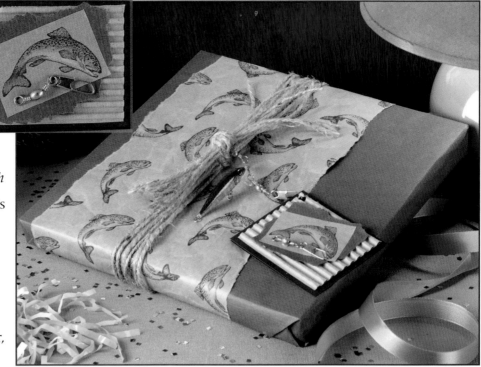

Custom design wrapping paper that's perfect for the occasion or recipient! First, wrap the gift in plain colored wrapping paper. Then, randomly stamp the image on kraft paper and color in each image. Tear the edges as was done here, or use patterned scissors. To make the tag, stamp a trout image on a scrap of kraft paper, color it and layer it on a scrap of colored wrapping paper. Glue it to the corrugated paper then on the cardstock. Fishing tackle creates a clever bit of masculine ribbon that links the tag to the twine knot. Be sure to remove the hook carefully.

Frog Gift Bag

*Tree Frog stamp, black pigment ink
clear embossing powder, heat tool
kraft gift bag
3" square of kraft paper, black checked tissue paper
brush markers: hunter green, light green, black
four 18" lengths of raffia
¼" hole punch, cardboard
tacky glue, scissors*

Keep the bag folded and insert a piece of cardboard. Stamp the Tree Frog image and emboss (see page 28) each one for texture and shine. Color each image as shown. To make the tag, fold the square of kraft paper in half and stamp the Frog. Cut around the image and draw a border around it with the black pen and punch a hole as shown. Handle the raffia strands as one and tie a shoestring bow (see page 41) with 2" loops and 4"-5" long tails around the handle. Thread one tail strand through the tag hole and knot it to secure. Insert the tissue paper.

Rose Gift wrap

Romantic Rose Small Bouquet stamp
clear embossing ink
gold embossing powder, heat tool
vellum Paper Pizazz™
pink blooming roses patterned
  Paper Pizazz™
1" wide gold mesh ribbon
three ½" long dried rose buds
gift box, tacky glue, scissors

Vellum paper lets the Paper Pizazz™ design show through and creates delicate gift wrap. Stamp an image on vellum and layer it on Paper Pizazz™ to combine a patterned design with your rubber stamps! Wrap the box in the blooming roses Paper Pizazz™. Repeatedly stamp and emboss (see page 28) the Small Bouquet image diagonally across the vellum paper and wrap it over the blooming roses Paper Pizazz™. Wrap the ribbon around the box and tie a shoe-string bow (see page 41) with 2" loops and 6" tails as shown. Glue the rosebuds to the bow center.

Silver Wedding Invitation

Rings Intertwined stamp
white pigment ink, white embossing powder, heat tool
8½"x11" vellum Paper Pizazz™, 5"x7" silver cardstock
15" of 1" wide silver mesh wire edged ribbon
¼" hole punch, scissors, newspaper
access to a computer and laser printer

A subtle hint of an image along the border may be all that's needed to carry the theme of the project. Use a computer to type in your message, then print it on the vellum Paper Pizazz™. Trim it to 6¾"x4¾" around the printing. Protect your work surface with newspapers and randomly stamp the Rings Intertwined image around the paper's border overlapping the edge. Emboss (see page 28) each image. Center the vellum Paper Pizazz™ on the silver cardstock, punch two holes 1" from the top and 1" apart. Thread each ribbon end through a hole, back to front, and tie a shoestring bow (see page 41) with 2" loops and 3" tails.

Rosebud Sachet Tag

Romantic Rose stamp
clear embossing ink & pen
gold embossing powder, heat tool
ivory cardstock: 3½"x1¾" piece, 1½" square piece
1¾" square of pink handmade paper
brush markers: pink, green
4 oz. of dried rose bud potpourri, 6" of gold cording
5½"x4½" sheer ivory sachet with ivory ribbon tie
⅛" hole punch

Embossed edges can provide a delicately elegant look. Simply draw along the torn edges of the cardstock square with the embossing pen. Sprinkle with gold powder and emboss (see page 28). Stamp and emboss the Rose image in the center. Color as shown. Fold the cardstock rectangle in half to make a tag. Tear the edges of the handmade paper, layer the elements and glue in place. Fill the sachet with potpourri and tie closed. Punch a hole in the corner, tie with cording and loop around the sachet neck.

English Rose Print

English Rose Collage stamp, black dye-based ink
6½"x5½" mauve paper, 5"x4" ivory cardstock
colored pencils: red, orange, yellow, peach, green,
   blue, purple
8"x10" gold embellished frame with an olive green mat
   board and a 5½"x4½" opening
scissors, tacky glue

This image is all one stamp which enables you to
create a beautiful print like this easily! Stamp the
English Rose Collage image on the ivory cardstock
and color it as shown. Glue it onto mauve paper
and center it inside the frame mat opening. Insert
the mat into the frame.

Rose Journal

Large Rose stamp, clear embossing ink & pen
gold embossing powder, heat tool
handmade paper: 3"x3½" rose, 3¾"x3½" mauve
2¾"x3¼" piece of ivory parchment paper
7¼"x5¼" ivory hardbound journal
watercolor pencils: pink, green
gold acrylic paint, old toothbrush
13" of 1" wide gold mesh ribbon, tacky glue

Torn edges give this journal a delicate, romantic
feeling. Stamp and emboss (see page 28) the Rose
image in the ivory paper center. Color it as shown.
Tear and emboss the edges. Tear the edges of the
remaining papers, layer as shown and glue. To

create the look of gold threads on the cover, dip the
toothbrush into gold paint and pull your thumb
across the bristles spattering the journal cover; let
dry. Fold the ribbon in half and glue the layered
papers over the ribbon in the center of the journal.

Peony Gift Box & Card

Peony stamp, brush markers: rose, green
2"x5¼"x2" white gift box
2"x3" piece of white cardstock
3¼"x 2¼" piece of olive green paper
24" of ⅝" wide pale yellow mesh ribbon
black pen, double stick tape, scissors, tracing paper, pencil

The entire image of a stamp doesn't have to fit on the project
to be effective. A hint of a leaf and the suggestion of a blossom
may be all that's needed to create a pretty design. Carefully
unfold the gift box and lie it flat, right side up. Color the
image with brush markers and randomly stamp the gift box.
Re-fold the box and secure it with double stick tape. Wrap
the box with ribbon and tie a shoestring bow (see page 41)
with 1½" loops and 2" tails. Stamp one Peony image onto the
small cardstock piece, glue it to the green paper and write the
gift recipient's name on it.

Balloon Present Giftwrap

Party Balloon stamp
black pigment ink, clear embossing powder, heat tool
white gloss-coated gift wrap paper
brush markers: green, blue, yellow, pink, dark pink
gift box, scissors, blue raffia

Brush markers create such vibrant colors when drawn on gloss-coated paper. Randomly angle the stamp to add excitement to this festive wrapping paper. Emboss (see page 28) the images to really make them pop! Color the Party Balloon images as shown and wrap the gift box in the paper. Cut the raffia in half, handle both strands as one and tie it around the gift making a shoestring bow (see page 41).

Wacky Cake Birthday Card

Wacky Cake stamp
black pigment ink
clear embossing powder
heat tool
5¼"x10½" white cardstock
black & white checked patterned Paper Pizazz™
brush markers: pink, green, dark pink
brayer
X-acto® knife, ruler, tacky glue
pencil with eraser
scissors

The absorbent quality of uncoated paper makes lightly colored brush markers look like watercolors. Use the cardstock to make a top folding birthday card (see page 41). Draw ⅛" wide green and ¹⁄₃₂" wide pink lines directly on the brayer roller and create a plaid pattern on the card front (see page 30). Draw and carefully cut out a 2½" square from the card front center. Cut four ⅛"x2½" and four ⅛"x5¼" strips of black & white checked Paper Pizazz™. Glue them around the outer card edges and to frame the window. Use a pencil to lightly trace the window onto the inside back of the card. Stamp the Wacky Cake inside the penciled square in the card and erase the pencil lines. Emboss it (see page 28), then color it in with brush markers.

Sunflower Card

Woodcut Sunflower stamp
black pigment ink
clear embossing powder, heat tool
ivory cardstock: 8¾"x5¾" piece, 3¾"x2½" piece
olive green paper: 2¾"x4" piece, 1"x5¾" strip
brush markers: olive green, hunter green, burgundy,
  yellow-orange
blue watercolor pencil, #2 round paintbrush
brayer, tacky glue, ruler
deckle patterned scissors, straight edged scissors

Images that have many detail lines create a well
textured, dimensional look when embossed. Stamp
the Woodcut Sunflower image on the small cardstock,
emboss it (see page 28) and paint the background
blue. Color the image with markers as shown. Use
straight edged scissors to cut around the image. Fold
the large cardstock to make a card (see page 41).
Draw ⅛" wide and 1/32" wide green bands on the brayer roller to create a plaid card front (see page 30).
Glue the green paper strip to the inside right edge of
the card and use the pattern edged scissors to cut a ½"
wide strip from the right card front edge so the green
strip shows. Mat the image on the green paper and
trim with patterned scissors. Glue to the card front.

Sunflower Clay Frame

Sunflower Design stamp
clear embossing ink
dark green polymer clay
cardboard: 2"x4" piece, 5½" square
acrylic paints: yellow, light green, rust
X-acto® knife, ruler
¼" wide flat paintbrush
rolling pin or 1" dowel
waxed paper, tacky glue

Polymer clay is a unique medium for rubber stamps
and provides a terrific look. Cover your work surface
with waxed paper. Roll the polymer clay to a ⅛"
thick, 6" square sheet. Ink the stamp with clear
embossing ink and press it randomly onto the clay
sheet. Cut a 5½" square and remove a 2½" square
from the center. Follow the manufacturer's
directions to bake the clay. Paint the Sunflower
images as shown. Cut a cardboard back ⅛" smaller
than the frame. Glue it to the frame back on three
sides, leaving the top open to slip a photo inside.
Glue the top ½" of the cardboard strip to the center
frame back for a frame stand.

Happy Birthday

Thanks Gratzi Danke! Arrigato
Thank You Merci ¡Gracias!
Arrigato Thanks
Merci Beaucoup

FROM THE GARDEN OF...

On Your Wedding Day

May my heart always be open to little birds who are the secret of living — e. e. cummings

Je t'aime Mukuirâréta
Gichhan Ti che cherzo
Tebi Ich Liebe Dich
za ljubar
i love you Te Quiero I Love!
Mukuirâréta Tibtimo Jatuk Cinta
Tebi za ljubar Ti Amo
Lief Zijn Voor Te Eu
Ti che cherzo Quiero i love you
Jatuk Je t'aime Tibtimo
Cinta I Love!

Bundle of Joy

Spring!

RUBBER STAMPEDE   Berkeley CA 94701

Earth Laughs in Flowers

Earth Laughs in Flowers
RUBBER STAMPEDE   Berkeley CA 94701

Love Out Loud

Bundle of Joy

Good Luck

Life is beautiful

Word Stamps

Stamps containing only words are the focus of this chapter. There are lots of sayings, phrases, greetings, and even a poem or two to choose from—and many different styles of letters. So if you want to be silly, serious, romantic or just plain fun, there's a word stamp that will fit your needs.

Send a warm fuzzy to someone close to your heart with the sentiment cards shown on the top of page 52. They're super easy to make, and with touching phrases like, "Love Out Loud," or "Eath laughs in flowers," you know they'll warm someone's heart.

Word stamps can be used for more than simply greeting cards! The candle holder projects at the top of page 54 incorporate word stamps into a collage. They make a statement of natural simplicity. A simply phrased word stamp can create the title to a photo album, or sum up the feelings expressed in a photograph as shown in the projects on page 55.

Word stamps can create a wonderful background for other stamped images like the clock face on page 57, or behind cherished photos such as the wedding photo book shown on page 56.

Word stamps are designed to successfully stamp on any surface from paper to wood to fabric—the letters remain crisp and legible no matter where you stamp them! From fun letters and basic surfaces (such as the gift tags on page 52) to fancy words and elegant textiles (like the silk pillow on page 56), word stamps remain effective in easily saying what you mean.

This chapter's background paper is from Paper Pizazz™ Handmade Papers

Watercolored Sentiment Cards

word stamps: "Life is Beautiful,"
  "Earth Laughs in Flowers,"
  "Love Out Loud,"
  "On Your Wedding Day"
black waterproof ink
watercolor paper
watercolors: green, blue, orange, tan,
  fuchsia, purple, turquoise
#2 liner paintbrush, scissors, ruler
new pencil with eraser, tacky glue

Word stamps easily express a
sentiment for any occasion.
Contemporary designs such as
these stripes, squares and dots
match any theme or emotion.

Cut three 7"x3½" and one 5"x7¼" piece of watercolor paper and fold
each to create a card (see page 41). For the circles, use the pencil to
lightly trace coins or circle templates and fill each in with watercolors.
Draw squares and stripes on the backgrounds as shown. Erase any
pencil lines when the paint dries. Use waterproof ink to stamp the
images. Layer some images on separate backgrounds for interest.

Colorful Gift Tags

"Fun to/from" stamp
dye-based inks: fuchsia, red, purple, teal, black
cardstock: white, goldenrod, magenta
colored self-adhesive reinforcements, pencil
¼" hole punch, string, scissors, tracing paper

The opaque quality of dye-based inks makes
them a good choice when stamping on
colored paper or cardstock. Because you
can't see through dye-based inks, the color
of paper doesn't affect the color of the ink.

Cut the tags (pattern on page 140) from
colored cardstock and punch a hole through
the tops as shown. Apply the reinforcements
for added color and tie strings to each. Stamp
each colored tag in a variety of contrasting colors
for gift tags with pizazz!

Whimsical Birthday Gift Tin

Whimsical Birthday Wishes
Stamp Collection
black dye-based ink
uncoated sticker paper
tin container with lid
brush markers: red, pink, blue
green, purple, orange
scissors

Sticker paper allows you to easily decorate any surface! Just stamp the sticker paper, cut it out and stick it on your project. Sticker paper is ideal for working on hard-to-stamp surfaces like this circular tin. Use brush markers to color all or parts of the images before adhering the paper to the tin.

Whimsical Birthday Card

Whimsical Birthday Wishes Stamp Collection
black pigment ink, clear embossing powder
black embossing pen, heat tool
white cardstock
brush markers: purple, blue, green, yellow,
  pink, fuchsia
ruler, Post-it® notes, tacky glue
scissors, X-acto® knife, foam mounting tape

The young, and the young at heart will love this whimsical birthday wish! Fold a 10¼"x7" piece of cardstock in half to make a card (see page 41). Mask (see page 29) the outer ⅜" and randomly stamp and emboss (see page 28) the candles. Remove the mask pieces and color the card edges green. Cut a free-form, wavy edged piece of cardstock for the center, draw a green border around it and use the embossing pen to draw and emboss a black outline as shown. Stamp and emboss "Happy Birthday" in the lower portion as shown and adhere it to the card front. Use the embossing pen to emboss decorative dots in the empty spaces. Stamp the birthday cake onto cardstock, emboss it and cut it out. Use the markers to color the images and draw over each letter of the word stamp. Use foam mounting tape or dots to adhere the cake to the card. Cut tiny pieces of foam mounting tape to support each candle flame, too.

Thank You Card

stamps: "Thank You," Sun, Bee, Heart, Tulip, Flower
black dye-based ink pad
white gloss-coated cardstock, black cardstock
1" square dye-based ink pads: blue, pink, green, yellow
X-acto® knife, ruler, scissors, white chalk

Trim the white cardstock to 4"x5". Cut out the center 3"x4" piece, and trim it to 2¾"x3¾". Stamp the word stamp in the middle and draw a pink border. Use the small ink pads as 1" square stamps to stamp a border of color around the cardstock frame. Let dry then stamp each image in black. Cut a 5½"x9" piece of black cardstock and fold in half to make a top-folding card. Glue both frame pieces to the card front. Write a personal message inside using chalk for a fun effect!

Candle Holders

stamps: Nature's Acorn, Nature's
*   Pomegranate*
pigment ink pads: blue, burgundy
handmade papers: white, brown,
*   burgundy, blue*
9" and 6" tall 3½" wide round glass
*   candle holders*
brush markers: orange, burgundy, green,
*   golden*
natural raffia
burgundy dried papaver sprigs
preserved eucalyptus sprigs: brown, green
decoupage glue, ¼" wide flat paintbrush

Stamp many blue Pomegranate images
onto blue paper. Stamp many burgundy
Acorn images onto burgundy paper.
Use the markers to color directly on the
stamps then stamp the Pomegranate
and Acorn stamps onto white paper.
Tear out all of the images. Tear the
brown paper into pieces. Collage (see
page 35) the Acorn images to the small
candle holder and the pomegranate
images to the large one. Wrap raffia
around each; tie the drieds into each
knot as shown.

Fleur de Lis Note Card

stamps: "Just A Note," Ornate Fleur de Lis
clear embossing ink & pen
gold embossing powder, heat tool
solid color papers: black, gold, olive green
6"x4¼" black corrugated paper
black with gold threads handmade card
acrylic paints: purple, olive, green, pink, dark green
12" of ½" wide black & white checked ribbon
gold photo corners, #0 round paintbrush, tacky glue
deckle patterned scissors, straight edge scissors

Basic collage techniques as shown on page 35
were used here to create this elegant card.
Acrylic paints offer a striking complement to
the stamped and embossed Fleur de Lis design.
Use an embossing pen to lay ink on the raised
strips of the corrugated paper. Cover it with
embossing powder and heat (see page 28) to
create this embossed striped background. Trim some of the elements
with patterned scissors to add variety and texture. Tie a shoestring
bow (see page 41) with 1½" loops and 3" tails and glue it above the
matted word stamp for a finishing touch.

Bundle of Joy Album

stamps: "Bundle of Joy," Baby Bear; black pigment ink
clear embossing powder, heat tool
Paper Pizazz™ patterned papers: blue pastel plaid,
  pastel dots on yellow
scrapbook album (with white paper cover)
uncoated sticker paper, buttons, bows, photograph
archival quality glue, watercolors: blue, yellow, brown
¼" wide flat paintbrush, foam mounting tape
ripple patterned scissors, straight edged scissors

Randomly stamp and emboss (see page 28) the
Bear at different angles for interest and variety.
Paint them, then paint a color block behind a few.
Paint a border of **x\/x\/x** to give the look of a
stitched patch as shown. Mat (see page 41) baby's
picture on the Paper Pizazz™ sheets as shown and
glue it to the cover. Cut out a stamped Bear image
and affix it with foam mounting tape to the corner
of the photo. Stamp the word stamp on sticker
paper and adhere it over the matted photo as
shown. Glue buttons and bows for added texture.

Bundle of Joy Frame

stamps: Baby Shoes, Baby Bottle, "Bundle of Joy"
black pigment ink, clear embossing powder, heat tool
8"x10" blue frame with ivory mat with an oval opening
watercolors: pink, yellow, blue, green
¼" wide flat paintbrush, blue colored pencil

Embossing ink doesn't absorb into uncoated paper, so
stamped letters, lines and details will stay sharp, even
on a paper mat. Stamp and emboss (see page 28) the
saying and images. Then use watercolors to highlight
the letters, paint background blocks behind a few
images and fill in color on others. Draw a border line
around the picture opening with the blue pencil.

Congratulations Puzzle Card

stamps: Baby Bear, Baby Bottle, "Fun Congratulations"
clear embossing powder, pigment inks: black, lavender
4"x6" blank puzzle card, Post-it® notes, ruler, heat tool
brush markers: blue, yellow, green, pink, brown

Stamp your greeting then create a fun background
behind the words. Image lines appear sharp and clean
when embossed—even if stamped on a broken
surface like this puzzle card. Mask (see page 29) a
1¼"x3½" frame in the center of the card. Then stamp

and emboss (see page 28) the Bear images to overlap
it. Color each in with markers. Remove the mask.
Stamp "Congratulations" and draw around the border
with the blue marker.

Forget Me Not Pillow

stamps: "Forget Me Not", Versailles Desk Set Stamp Trio
gold fabric ink
9" square fabric swatches (we used silk): 2 purple, 1 ivory
26" of 2" wide purple organza ribbon, fleur de lis button
access to a sewing machine, matching thread, needle
2 oz. of polyester fiberfill, scissors, straight pins

Create a pillow with word stamps that carries a special message. Refer to page 38 for stamping fabric before beginning. Stamp the fabric before you cut it. Repeatedly stamp the "Forget me not" image on the ivory fabric and the Fleur de Lis on one purple piece. Cut the stamped fabric squares in half diagonally to make triangles. Pin one side of an ivory and purple triangle, right sides together. Stitch leaving a ½" seam allowance and unfold. Repeat. Pin the long sides together, right sides together, then stitch, leaving a ½" seam allowance, to make a square. Unfold. Cut the ribbon into four 6" lengths. Lay the two fabric squares right sides together then pin one ribbon length in the center of each side. Being careful to not catch the ribbon ends, stitch all four sides, leaving a ½" seam allowance and a 3" opening. Turn right side out, stuff and stitch the opening closed. Tie the ribbons and sew the button to the center.

Wedding Photo Book

"On Your Wedding Day" stamp
pale orange pigment ink
29"x7" piece of ivory paper
salmon cardstock
two 5¼"x7¼" pieces of cardboard
¼ yard of dark peach raw silk fabric
28" of 2" wide pearlescent sheer ribbon
archival quality glue, ruler, scissors
square, rectangle, oval templates
5 photographs

Repeatedly stamp at an angle on the ivory paper to make a patterned background. Cut two 7"x9" fabric pieces to wrap over cardboard fronts, fold excess around the backs and miter each corner. Use glue to secure. Cut two 5"x7" pieces of cardstock. Fold 2" of the ivory paper in widthwise, then fan-fold the remaining paper every 5", ending with a 2" fold. Glue one of each 2" fold to the back of a cover piece and glue a piece of cardstock over it to secure. Use the template to trim photos, mat (see page 41) on salmon cardstock and glue one to each book page. Close the book, wrap with the ribbon and tie a shoestring bow with 2½" loops and 4" tails.

To miter a corner: Fold the corner over, then fold in the top and side.

Peony Photo Frame

stamps: Peony, "May My Heart…"
clear embossing ink, gold embossing powder, heat tool
5"x7" frame with ivory mat
watercolors: pink, green
Post-it® notes
paintbrushes: #0 liner, ¼" wide flat

Stamp a frame mat to echo the theme of the photo the frame will hold. Mix one part water with one part pink watercolor paint then brush it over the mat before stamping to create a soft background for the images. Stamp and emboss (see page 28) the Peony. Mask (see page 29) the Peony images then stamp and emboss the word image. Use watercolors to paint the Peonies as shown.

Rose Decoupage Clock

stamps: Rose, French Frame
black crafter's ink, black pigment ink
clear embossing ink, gold embossing powder, heat tool
white paper
9½"x5¾"x2½" unfinished wood clock
clock works to fit
acrylic paints: pink, ivory, green, metallic gold
paintbrushes: ¼" wide flat , #0 liner
scissors, antique medium, soft cloth
water-based sealer, decoupage glue

Prepare the wood (see page 36). Paint the clock front ivory and the remaining clock gold. Use pigment ink to stamp and emboss (see page 28) three Rose images on white paper. Dilute (one part paint to one part water) the pink and green paints then paint the images as shown; let them dry and cut out. Isolate (see page 29) the word portion of the French Frame image and randomly stamp the clock front using black crafter's ink. Trim the Rose images so all three will fit then decoupage (see page 34) them to the clock front. Brush the antique medium on the clock and wipe off with the cloth. Let it dry. Seal. Follow the instructions to assemble the clock works.

Broad Surface Stamps

Broad surface stamps are the exact opposite of an outline stamp yet offer the same versatility and colorful results. Rather than having the outline of an image, they have the image without an outline. Simply put, they have a large area of flat rubber which gives the design. Brilliant color designs can be made by using brush markers to color the rubber die before stamping.

Broad surface stamps employ the concept of negative space to provide detail lines with an absence of ink. The tribal stamps used on the leather frames shown at the bottom of page 65 offer a great example of this.

Broad surface stamps are effective on a variety of surfaces. The simplicity of most broad surface stamps makes them a great choice for velvet embossing as shown at the bottom of page 62. Or, use them with Liquid Appliqué™ for a beautiful look like the lampshade shown at the top of page 60. The large image surface gives wonderful results when embossed in colorful pigment inks like the images in the calendar project at the bottom of page 64. The pliability of the foam handle makes them ideal for stamping on rough or curved surfaces such as a ceramic plate (shown at the top of page 64).

Broad surface stamps offer stampers a way to make a bold graphic statement. As you'll see in this chapter, broad surface stamps provide an excellent beginning for lots of wonderful looks.

This chapter's background paper is from Paper Pizazz™ Handmade Papers.

Faux Cast Paper Lampshade

Duet Hibiscus Stamp Set
light gray brush marker
watercolor paper, lampshade kit
watercolors: pink, yellow, green
white Liquid Appliqué™
¼" wide pink gimp braid
¼" wide flat paintbrush
heat tool, scissors, tacky glue

Follow the manufacturer's instructions to cut the lampshade using the watercolor paper. Color the Hibiscus image with the gray marker and stamp the lampshade three times as shown. Squeeze Liquid Appliqué™ to cover each entire image and let it dry overnight. Use the heat tool on the Appliqué™ until it puffs up and resembles embossed paper. Paint the images with watercolors. Wrap the paper around the lampshade base and glue the seam to secure. Glue the braid around the top and bottom edges of the lampshade.

Pillow & Baby Announcement

stamps: Little Lamb, Little Bunny, Little Chick, "Announcing"
blue fabric ink, pigment inks: blue, pink, yellow
two 6" square white doilies with yellow trim
5" square white card, blue paper
pastel dots patterned Paper Pizazz™
nine ¼"-½" wide assorted colored buttons
1¾ yard of ⅛" wide yellow satin ribbon, needle, thread
1 oz. of polyester fiberfill, ⅛" hole punch, tacky glue
scallop patterned scissors, straight edged scissors

For the pillow: Refer to page 38 for stamping on fabric before beginning. Use the fabric ink to stamp the Lamb in one doily center. Sew the buttons around it. Place the doilies wrong sides together and weave the ribbon through the center openings on three sides. Stuff it with fiberfill then continue weaving until the square is closed. Knot the ends. Sew or glue a 12" ribbon length for a hanger.

For the announcement: Cut the pastel dots Paper Pizazz™ to fit and glue to the card front. Randomly stamp pink Bunnies, blue Lambs and yellow Chicks. Stamp the word image onto the pastel dots Paper Pizazz™, trim to 4⅛"x2" and mat (see page 41) it on blue. Cut with scallop scissors ⅛" larger. Punch holes around the border and thread ribbon through, tying a shoestring bow with 1" loops and 2" tails in the top center. Glue to the card front, mat it on blue and trim with scallop scissors ⅛" larger.

Rose Bud Gift Set

stamps: Whimsical Rose Stem, Bouquet of Roses, Rosehead,
* "Wishing you…"*
brush markers: pink, green, purple, black
white gloss-coated cardstock gift box with a window
white gloss-coated cardstock, green paper
black & white checked patterned Paper Pizazz™
9 " of ½" wide black with white dots grosgrain ribbon
scissors, tacky glue, pencil, Post-it® notes

Create a great matching look using three similar stamps. **For the birthday card:** Cut a 6"x9" piece of cardstock and make a top-folding card (see page 41). Randomly stamp the Rosehead image on the card front. Use the black marker to make dots in the empty areas. Cut a ¼" wide wavy line from the front card flap. Cut a ¾"x6" wide green strip and glue it inside the lower back card. Cut a ⅛" wide black & white checked Paper Pizazz™ strip and glue to the

lower green strip. Stamp the word stamp on cardstock, draw a wavy border around it and cut out. Draw a black and purple border around it then glue it to the card center. Use the ribbon to tie a shoestring bow with ½" loops and 1½" tails. Glue it in the center of the card top.

For the box: Lay the flattened gift box on a hard surface; mask (see page 29) the window. Use the Rose Stem image to randomly stamp the box. Cut Paper Pizazz™ patterned paper to fit each side of the box handle and glue in place. Fold the box.

For the note card: Fold a 5¼"x3" piece of cardstock to open on the right. Stamp the Bouquet image in the center and make black dots in the empty areas. Cut away ¼" on the right front flap in a wavy pattern. Glue a ¾" wide green strip to the inside back card with a ⅛" wide black and white checked Paper Pizazz™ strip glued along the outside edge.

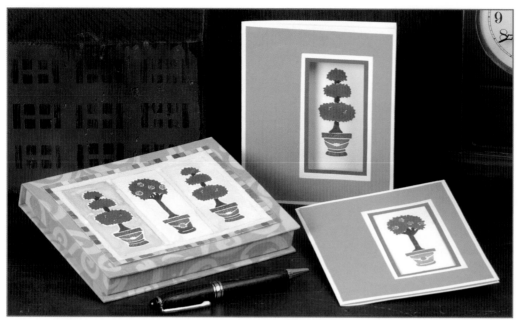

Topiary Stationery Box & Cards

*stamps: Orange Topiary,
    Tree Topiary*
*pigment inks: blue, purple, orange,
    green, brown*
watercolor paper, stationery box
two 6¼"x5" white matte cards
*solid color papers: olive, purple,
    blue*
*watercolors: purple, green, blue,
    pink, red, orange, olive, fuchsia*
¼" wide flat paintbrush, ruler
X-acto® knife, scissors, tacky glue

For the box: Measure the box lid surface and cut the watercolor paper ½" smaller on each side. Apply ink to the appropriate portion of each stamp and press the Topiary images on the paper as shown. Use watercolors to paint light blocks of color around each image and to create a colorful border around the paper edges. Glue the paper to the lid top.

For the cards: Cut a 2"x4" window in each card front flap for the Tree Topiary image to show through. Open one card and glue a 3"x5" piece of blue paper on the inside front flap to cover the window. Cut a window in the blue paper ⅛"-¼" smaller than the card window. Close the card, apply ink to the appropriate portion of the stamp and press the Tree image through the window onto the inside card back. Cut the olive paper to 4¾"x5" and cut a window ⅛" larger than the card window. Glue to the card front. Repeat for the purple card using the Orange Topiary stamp and purple paper.

Velvet Album Cover

stamps: Decorative Swirl, Bold Berry Branch
velvet: 9"x10" piece of gold, 18"x10" piece of blue
two 12"x9" pieces of cardboard
two 11½"x8¾" pieces of blue cardstock
four gold grommets & tool
1 yard of ³⁄₁₆" wide gold cording
20" of ½" wide gold ribbon
three ¾" wide gold ribbon roses with green leaves
iron, ironing board, spray bottle with water
fabric glue, scissors, ¼" hole punch, filler paper

Velvet emboss (see page 39) the Swirl stamp onto the gold velvet and the Berry Branch onto the blue velvet. Lay the cardboard pieces side by side as an open book with the spine in the center of the gold velvet. Fold the excess over the top of each cover piece and glue to secure. Cut the blue velvet in half for two 9"x10" pieces and wrap one piece around each exposed cover end. Fold the excess over the cover, miter (see page 56) the corners and glue to secure. Glue the ribbon to cover the velvet seam. Glue each cardstock piece to cover the fabric edges inside the cover. Punch two holes 4" apart through the left end of the filler paper. Insert it into the album. Follow the manufacturer's directions to use the tool to insert the grommets. Thread the cording through from back to front and tie in a shoestring bow (see page 41) with 3" loops and tails. Glue the ribbon roses to the gold ribbon.

Aspen Leaf Gift Bag

Aspen Leaf stamp
clear embossing ink
embossing powders: gold, verdigris
kraft gift bag, copper sheet metal
light green brush marker
24-gauge gold wire
copper tissue paper, scissors
heat tool, awl, long tongs
cardboard, wire cutters

Keep the bag folded and insert a piece of cardboard. Randomly stamp and emboss (see page 28) gold Leaf images on the bag. Color each image light green. Stamp two verdigris Leaf images on the sheet metal, hold the metal with the tongs and emboss. Cut out and punch a hole in each leaf stem base with the awl. Coil the wire around the marker, remove and wrap around one bag handle base to drape down the bag like vines. Poke one wire end through each leaf hole and twist to secure. Insert the tissue.

Thank You Card

stamps: "Elegant Thank You", Bamboo
clear embossing ink
verdigris embossing powder, heat tool
copper sheet metal
5⅜"x5¼" sage green card, bronze paper
20" of ½" wide pearl green satin ribbon
deckle patterned scissors, tacky glue
straight edged scissors, long tongs

Stamp and emboss (see page 28) the "Thank You" image on the left side of the bronze paper. Cut it ⅛" smaller and glue it to the card front. Stamp the Bamboo image twice vertically on the sheet metal, hold the metal with the tongs and emboss. Cut out with the patterned scissors and glue to the right card front. Open the card and tie the ribbon in a shoestring bow (see page 41) with 1" loops and 2" tails around the card spine.

Dragonfly Tile Collage

Dragonfly stamp, pigment inks: black, green, gold
clear embossing powder
gold Pearl-EX pigment powder
2" square of corrugated cardboard
4¼"x6" piece of black corrugated paper
solid color papers: black, metallic gold
5"x6" piece of antique gold handmade paper
5"x7" gold frame (remove the glass), scissors, tacky glue
⅛" wide flat paintbrush, 4 strands of gold bullion thread

Press the green pigment ink pad onto the cardboard square to cover it with ink. Sprinkle embossing enamel powder over the inked cardboard, then sprinkle on gold Pearl-EX pigment powder and emboss (see page 28). Repeat 3-4 times. Apply black ink to the Dragonfly image, use the heat tool to heat up the embossed enamel on the square then press the stamp into the warm enamel. Carefully lift the stamp off and let it cool and dry thoroughly. Wad up, then smooth out, the gold paper. Tear the antique gold handmade paper in a free-form shape. Cut a 2¾" black paper square and paint gold stripes with the paintbrush. Collage (see page 35) the elements, including the bullion, onto the crinkled gold paper. Trim the collage to 5"x7" and insert it into the frame.

Turnip Plate

Turnip Decorative stamp
ceramic glazes: green, blue, red, orange
10" wide bisque dinner plate
paintbrushes: ½" wide, #2 round
foam sponges
access to a kiln—call a ceramic studio in the
yellow pages for a location near you

Refer to page 37 for stamping on ceramics before beginning. Apply red and green ceramic glazes to the Turnip stamp with foam sponges and stamp onto the plate center. Paint a second coat of glaze onto the stamped image. Paint a blue glaze around the image making a free-form wavy border. Leave a wavy strip of plate unglazed to create a white border. Paint the edges orange. Add red stripes or dots around the plate for more interest. Have the plate glazed and fired in a kiln by a professional.

Calendar Cards

stamp sets: Duet Present, Duet Leaf, Duet Heart, Duet Hibiscus (choose additional images to represent each calendar month)
black pigment ink, clear embossing powder, heat tool
gloss-coated sticker paper, white cardstock, scissors
Paper Pizazz™ patterned papers: red & white plaid, golden argyle, pink hearts on blue, pink embossed daisies (choose additional papers to represent each calendar month)
brush markers: pink, purple, yellow, red, green, orange, mauve
5"x7" acrylic stand-up frame
access to a computer and laser printer

Use a future calendar for reference and be sure to leave plenty of space between the month and the days for the stamp images. Load the printer with Paper Pizazz™ and print a calendar page with appropriate numbering for each month of the year. Stamp and emboss (see page 28) the images onto sticker paper. Color each with brush markers and cut around each image. Remove the backing and press the images onto each calendar page. Glue each page to cardstock and cut to 5"x7". Slip the current month's page into the frame for display.

Gold Leaf Candle

Large Fleur de Lis stamp
3½"x6"x2½" blue pillar candle
gold leaf & adhesive kit, ½" wide flat paintbrush
8 gold tacks, clear acrylic sealer, foam sponges

Read the manufacturer's instructions on the gold leafing kit before beginning. Brush sealer onto the candle center front. Apply the gold leaf adhesive to the stamp with a foam sponge and impress the image onto the candle. Let it dry. Apply the gold leafing to the adhesive and gently sponge away any excess. Embellish the candle with tacks as was done here, or ribbons and charms if desired.

Leather Tribal Frames

stamps: Aztec Frog, Border Tile, Native, Primitive Lizard,
* Spiral Gecko, Aztec Swirl*
dye-based inks: red, green, purple, yellow
17"x5½" strip of tan smooth leather, white mat board
leather glue, X-acto® knife, ruler, pencil
photographs, tracing paper, scissors

Cut the leather strip into the following frames: one 7"x5½" frame with a 4¼"x2¾" center opening, one 6"x5" frame with a 2¼"x3¼" center opening and one 4" square frame with a 2" square center opening. Stamp the images onto the leather frames as shown and let the ink dry. Cut the white mat board to fit each frame and glue it to the backs leaving the tops open to slip in a photo. Trace the pattern on page 141 and cut a mat board support piece for each frame. Glue to support the frames.

Creating A Background

The previous three chapters have introduced the most common types of rubber stamps—outline stamps, word stamps and broad surface stamps. In this chapter and the next, you'll see different ways to use these stamps. This chapter focuses on how these stamps can create beautiful backgrounds for a variety of projects.

Word stamps create wonderful backgrounds that can really add to the project's design. The flowing scripted letters of the poem embossed on the purple gift bag (shown at the top of page 68) create an elegant background that matches well with the ornate pear image also used. The open, flowing letters of the background word image used on the anniversary gift bag (bottom of page 68) coordinates with the romantic theme.

Page 69 shows wonderful examples of how effective a broad surface or outline stamp can be when used to create a background. The randomly stamped leaves support the theme of a vegetable garden as suggested by the foreground stamps. The outline stamp used on the journal at the page bottom is hinted at in partial images all throughout the background—this keeps the eye roaming the design as it seeks to complete an image.

Embossed outline stamps create lots of deep texture as shown on the journal at the bottom of page 70. At the same time, embossed broad surface stamps add texture and shine to frame backgrounds as shown on page 72.

The backgrounds shown in the projects on page 73 are completely different—though they were made with the same stamp. The top example embossed the print onto crinkled paper, while the lower example impressed the print into a thin sheet of polymer clay. Both results are equally striking.

Creating a background for your project is simple, and no matter what type of stamp you use, there are lots of ideas in this chapter!

This chapter's background paper is from Paper Pizazz™ Handmade Papers.

Ornate Pear Gift Bag

stamps: Ornate Pear, "May my heart…"
clear embossing ink & pen, gold embossing powder, heat tool
purple gift bag, cardboard, silver tissue paper
4½"x3" piece of black cardstock
3½"x4½" piece of handmade pale blue paper
3½"x5½" piece of light green construction paper
acrylic paints: light green, dark green, goldenrod, teal,
  turquoise, pink
tacky glue, #0 round paintbrush

Word stamps create an effective background without detracting from the focal image. Keep the bag folded and insert a piece of cardboard. Repeatedly stamp and emboss (see page 28) the "May my heart…" image onto the bag front. Stamp and emboss the Ornate Pear onto the cardstock and carefully paint it as shown. Tear the edges. To emboss the edges, draw around the edges with the embossing pen, sprinkle with gold powder and heat. Tear the edges of the other papers and layer them to create a collage (see page 35). Open the bag and insert the tissue paper.

Anniversary Gift Bag

stamps: Elegant "Happy Anniversary", Raspberry Collage
pigment inks: red, black
clear embossing powder, heat tool
3¼"x3½" piece of white cardstock, white gift bag
solid color papers: 3¾"x4¼" green, 3¾"x4¼" mustard,
  3½"x4" red
watercolors: yellow, green, red, dark green, brown
16" of 1" wide green mesh ribbon
#0 round paintbrush, cardboard, tacky glue
deckle patterned scissors, straight edged scissors

Word stamps used as background images subtly convey the meaning of the occasion. Keep the bag folded and insert a piece of cardboard. Repeatedly stamp the "Happy Anniversary" image in red ink at an angle on the bag. Stamp and emboss (see page 28) the Raspberry Collage image in black ink on the cardstock. Use the watercolors to color in the image. Tear the edges of the stamped cardstock and the red paper. Trim ¼" off the mustard paper with patterned scissors. Glue the papers as shown then glue to the bag front. Use the ribbon to tie a shoestring bow (see page 41) with 2" loops and 4" tails and glue it as shown.

Veggie Gift Bag

Decorative foam stamps: Leaf Cluster, Tomato, Eggplant, Artichoke
stamping paints: red, green, purple, dark green
kraft gift bag, 5¼"x6" piece of corrugated cardboard
solid color papers: 8"x10" white, 6"x6½" red, 6½"x7" purple
6 strands of 18" long green raffia
tissue papers: red checked, lime green
deckle patterned scissors, straight edged scissors, tacky glue

Repeat an image related to your focal stamp theme to create a background. These Leaf Cluster images are perfect for this garden veggie bag. Keep the bag folded and insert a piece of cardboard. Randomly stamp green Leaf Cluster images to cover the bag front. Apply paint to the appropriate portions of each image and stamp one of each vegetable image onto white paper. Cut around each and layer them onto the corrugated paper. Mat (see page 41) on red trimmed with patterned scissors and then on purple. Glue the piece to the bag front. Handle the raffia strands as one and tie a shoestring bow with 2"-4" loops and 7"-10" tails around one handle side. Open the bag and insert the tissue.

Lavender Journal Collage

Lavender stamp, black waterproof ink
3"x4" piece of ivory cardstock
two 8"x5½" pieces of corrugated cardboard
solid color papers: olive, teal, red
watercolors: purple, green, lavender
sprigs of dried lavender, 1⅔" yard natural twine
#0 round paintbrush, tacky glue, ¼" hole punch
filler paper, scissors

Separate the stamped background from the focal image with collage papers. **For the Journal:** Cut the filler paper to 7¾"x5¼". Insert them between the cardboard pieces. Punch two holes 3" apart ½" in from the left end through all the papers and the covers. Cut four 12" lengths of twine. Handle them as one and thread them through the holes from back to front. Tie a knot to bind the journal. Stamp the image on the ivory paper and color it in. Randomly stamp the image on the red paper, then tear it to fit on the journal cover. Tear the other papers in a similar fashion and glue them on the cover. Bind the lavender sprigs with twine and glue them to the cover.

Vellum Invitation

stamps: Lemon Blossom, "Invitation"
white pigment ink, clear embossing powder, heat tool
white card, mauve paper, vellum Paper Pizazz™
brush markers: green, yellow
white photo corners
deckle patterned scissors, straight edged scissors, tacky glue

Next to a single, colored image, uncolored images will create a subtle background. Randomly stamp and emboss (see page 28) the Lemon Blossom image on the vellum Paper Pizazz™. Color one image as shown on the back side of the vellum. Cut the vellum to fit the card front and glue it in place. Stamp and emboss the word stamp on vellum paper then trim using patterned scissors. Glue it onto the mauve paper then use the patterned scissors to trim the edges. Glue it to the card under the colored blossom image with photo corners.

Thinking of You Card

stamps: Romantic Flower Basket, "Thinking of You"
clear embossing ink, gold embossing powder, heat tool
pink parchment note card, vellum Paper Pizazz™
brush markers: blue, green, pink, mauve
18" of ½" wide gold mesh ribbon
Victorian patterned scissors, straight edged scissors
ruler, ⅛" hole punch

Stamp a card with an image, then cover it with vellum Paper Pizazz™ to create a soft background. Turn the card so it opens at the bottom. Use the pink marker to draw a ½" wide strip along the card bottom. Repeatedly stamp and emboss (see page 28) the word stamp on the card front. Cut the vellum Paper Pizazz™ to the same size as the card. Fold it to cover the card then stamp and emboss one Flower Basket image on the lower front. Color the image on the back side. Trim ¼" off the lower front with patterned scissors. Punch two holes 2" apart in the card top, thread the ribbon through the holes and tie it in a shoestring bow (see page 41) with 2" loops and 5" tails.

Celestial Journal

stamps: Starry Night, Woodcut Sun
clear embossing ink, gold embossing powder, heat tool
copper paper, 3"x3" copper sheeting, 4½"x6½" journal
3¼" square of black corrugated paper, copper bullion threads
pinking patterned scissors, straight edged scissors, tacky glue, long tongs

Create a textured background with embossed images. Cut an 11"x7½" piece of copper paper. Stamp and emboss (see page 28) the Starry Night image to cover it. Wrap the paper to cover the journal and miter the corners (see page 56). Glue to secure. Stamp the Sun image on the copper sheeting. Hold it with tongs and emboss. Let it cool. Trim with pinking shears. Glue to the corrugated paper, catching three or four pieces of bullion to extend from between them. Glue the piece to the cover.

Vintage Cigar Box

stamps: Vintage Pocket Watch, Vintage
*   Key, Newspaper Background,*
*   Antique ABC's peg set*
black crafter's ink
white paper
letters patterned Paper Pizazz™
unfinished wood cigar box
ivory acrylic paint
antiquing medium
old cloth, sandpaper
decoupage glue, clean cloth, scissors
½" wide flat paintbrush

Its okay to leave the background plain so your stamped
images get all the attention! Paint the box ivory; let dry. Stamp many
Watch, Key and Newspaper images onto white paper. Stamp out "Timeless
Treasures" as shown. Cut out whole letter images from the patterned Paper
Pizazz™. Tear around the stamped images. Collage (see page 35) the images
onto the box. Stamp some images directly on the box in empty spaces. Brush
on the antiquing medium, wipe with the old cloth and let dry. Apply a second
coat in places for a darker appearance to create an aged look. Lightly sand the
edges for a worn look.

Letters paper from Paper
Pizazz™ book *Black &*
White Photos, HOTP 3015

Vintage Memory Page

stamps: Vintage Ship, Vintage Plane, Vintage Train,
*   Journaling Banner, Large Monogram Alphabet Set*
gray pigment ink, black & blue dye-based inks
acid-free white sticker paper, black photo corners
acid-free papers: two 12"x12" pink, two gray
photographs, memorabilia, 3-ring binder, scissors
acid-free sheet protectors, archival quality glue

Cut the photos to remove excess background and
affix each to gray paper with the photo corners. Trim
⅛"-¼" around each photo. Here, the map of France
further indicates where the vacation was taken. Tear
the edges keeping with the vintage theme of the
pages. Arrange the elements onto the pages until you
like the placement, overlapping some elements to add
interest. Cut out the Banner image and adhere it in
an empty area. Slip each page into a sheet protector
and then into a 3-ring binder.

These stamp images
create a wonderful
background for
vacation photos! To
ensure your album
pages remain acid-
free, color copy any
memorabilia onto
acid-free paper. Stamp
the Banner image
onto sticker paper.
Stamp the letters with
blue ink to spell out
where the vacation
took place. Randomly
stamp gray Vintage
images to cover both
pink papers. Let dry.

Metal Heart Frame

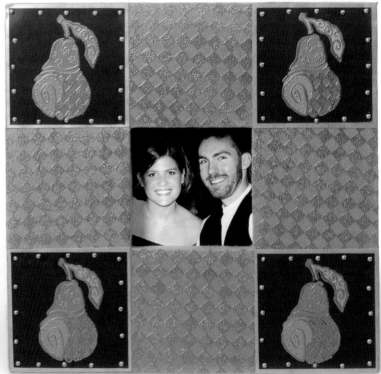

stamps: Heart, Checkerboard
clear embossing ink & pen
copper & gold embossing powder, heat tool
metal sheeting
cardstock: metallic gold, black
5"x7" copper mat with oval opening
scissors, tacky glue, ruler, long tongs
tracing paper, pencil

The Checkerboard image makes a great background for this frame. Stamp and emboss (see page 28) a gold Checkerboard image across the entire mat. Stamp four copper Hearts on the metal sheeting. Hold it with tongs and emboss. Let it cool. Cut out each Heart to a 1¼" square. Mat (see page 41) each on black cardstock trimming ³⁄₁₆" larger. Use the embossing pen to draw and emboss four gold dots around the black corners for "nails." Glue one in each mat corner. Cut the gold cardstock to 5¼"x7¼". Glue three sides of the mat board to the cardstock leaving the top open to slip in a photo. Trace the pattern on page 141 and cut a frame support from cardstock. Glue the support to the frame back.

Whimsical Pear Frame

stamps: Whimsical Pear, Checkerboard
clear embossing ink, gold embossing powder, heat tool
12"x12" green handmade paper
9"x9"x½" corrugated frame with a 3" square opening
cardstock: black, metallic gold
acrylic paints: turquoise, pink, green, lime, lavender
many small gold head tacks, #0 round paintbrush
decoupage glue, scissors

Embossing on handmade paper creates a wonderfully rich background of fuzzy paper and shiny, smooth shapes! Cover the frame with green paper using decoupage glue (see page 34). Let dry. Stamp and emboss (see page 28) the Checkerboard image diagonally to create diamonds over the entire frame surface. Stamp and emboss four Pear images on black paper. Carefully paint the images with acrylic paints. Cut each out in a 3" square. Mat (see page 41) them onto gold cardstock and glue one to each frame corner. Press the tacks in around each Pear mat as shown for added texture. Glue or tape a photo behind the frame to show through the opening.

Tiger Print Picture

stamps: Tiger Print, Bengal Tiger
black pigment ink, clear embossing powder, heat tool
solid color papers: white, rust, black
black note card, natural handmade paper
brush markers: orange, yellow
black acrylic paint, black photo corners
12" of natural twine, tacky glue
Post-it® notes, toothbrush
deckle patterned scissors, straight edged scissors

The many backgrounds of spattered, torn,
ragged, crinkled and contrasting papers
creates a primal sense for this roaring
card! To give a crinkled look, wad up the
rust paper then spread it out flat. Repeatedly
stamp and emboss (see page 28) the Tiger Print image
to cover it. Cut it to 6"x4⅝" and save the scraps. Stamp and
emboss the Bengal image on white paper, color it in and mask it (see
page 29). To lightly spatter the white paper, dip the dampened toothbrush
into black paint and pull your thumb across the bristles. Remove the mask. Use
patterned scissors to trim it to 3⅞"x2⅛". Affix it to rust paper with photo corners
then trim the rust paper edges using the patterned scissors and glue it to black
paper. Tear the edges of the handmade paper and some Tiger Print scraps from
above. Collage (see page 35) the elements onto the black card. Cut three 4" lengths
of twine, handle as one and tie into a knot. Glue above the Bengal as shown.

Aztec Clay Frame

stamps: Tiger Print, Tribal Pot
black pigment ink
rust colored polymer clay
X-acto® knife, rolling pin, tacky glue, pencil
cardboard, ruler, wax paper, tracing paper, scissors

Though it's the same image as above, used
with the Tribal Pot, this background conveys
an Aztec feeling reminiscent of the Plains.
Cover your work surface with wax paper.
Roll the clay to an ⅛" thick, 5½" square
sheet. Repeatedly impress the Tiger Print
image into it using black ink. Remove the
center 2½" square and stamp the Tribal Pot
with black ink. Cut around the image.
Follow all of the manufacturer's
instructions to bake the pieces.
Glue the Tribal Pot to the
frame. Glue a 5½" cardboard
square to the frame back on
three sides leaving the top open
to slip in a photo. Trace the pattern
on page 141 and cut a frame support
from cardboard. Glue it to the frame back.

Creating A Focal Point

Like the previous chapter, this chapter isn't about a style of stamp (like the outline or broad surface stamp). Instead it's about a variety of techniques showing how a stamp, any stamp, can be used to create a focal point. It's easy to find the focal point of a project—it's where your eye goes first. Usually it's the largest image on the project and often it's the most colorful image, too.

There are lots of textures and gingham sizes on the balsa angel ornament gift bag on page 79. But, your eye quickly rests on the focal point angel stamp. At the bottom of the same page the muted hearts provide a great background for the card but the bright red heart in the middle easily captures your attention.

Color is used to draw attention in the rose box on page 80. The images on the box sides blend into the pink wash making the colors seem muted and pale. However, the focal image on the box top, surrounded by a contrasting ivory background, visually pops off the lid with deeper pinks and greens. The rose is a true focal point as your eye immediately goes to it first!

Can a tiny stamp be a focal point? Look at the album on page 77 and notice the very wide border given around the Baby Shoes stamp. You know exactly where to look for the focal point.

Whether your project is simple or visually busy, if there is a strong focal point, as created by color, placement or size, your design will be a success!

This chapter's background paper is from Paper Pizazz™ Handmade Papers.

Baby's Beary Mobile

stamps: Ballerina Bear, Beary Bear, Beary Swinging on the
    Moon, Bedtime Bear, Cowboy Beary, Beary & Friends,
    Beary Surprise
black pigment ink, clear embossing powder, heat tool
five 2" square white gloss-coated cardstock gift boxes
white gloss-coated cardstock
brush markers: brown, pink, red, lavender, yellow,
    light blue, maroon, tan, navy
1⅓ yard of ⅜" wide light blue satin picot ribbon, ruler
tacky glue, scissors, tracing paper, pencil, black fine-tip pen

Create a fun focal object for baby's room with these
bear outline stamps. Lay a box flat then stamp and
emboss (see page 28) one Bear image on all four sides
and the bottom flap. Use the pen and ruler to draw a
1½" square on each box panel and color it yellow.
Repeat using a different stamp for each box. Notice
the lowest box with the Moon stamp does not have
a yellow block behind the image. Color each box
border and image as shown. Fold the boxes. Trace
the pattern on page 140 and cut the mobile top from
cardstock. Stamp and color the mobile top. Draw a ¼"
triangle border around each image as shown. Cut four
6" and one 9" ribbon length for the center box. Poke a
hole in each box top. Thread the ribbon through the
hole and tie a knot on the inside. Poke holes in the
mobile top as indicated on the pattern then thread one
ribbon end through each hole and knot to suspend the
boxes. Fold and glue the top as indicated, securing a
15" ribbon length in the top to suspend it.

Pansy Collage Card

Pansy stamp
clear embossing ink pad & pen, gold embossing powder, heat tool
cardstock: 10"x5" white, 4" square of ivory
10"x5" piece of purple with white dots patterned Paper Pizazz™
3"x2" piece of gold metallic paper, 4" square of olive green paper
4" square of purple handmade paper
watercolors: purple, green, yellow
gold bullion threads, tacky glue
deckle patterned scissors, straight edged scissors

Large images easily create a strong focal point. Refer to page
41 to fold the white cardstock into a card and cover with
purple with white dots Paper Pizazz™. Stamp and emboss
(see page 28) the Pansy onto the ivory cardstock. Paint it
then tear the edges. Draw around the torn edges with the
embossing pen, sprinkle with gold powder and emboss. Tear
the edges of the green and purple papers. Crinkle, flatten
then trim the edges of the gold paper with patterned
scissors. Collage (see page 35) the elements onto the card.
Glue a few pieces of bullion to extend upward from under
the pansy layer.

Bunny Pillow

Bunny Decorative stamp
stamping paints: pink, green
5¼" square of white fabric
10"x20" piece of lavender fabric
*   with white dots*
twelve ⅝" wide yellow buttons
#1 liner paintbrush
6 oz. of polyester fiberfill, thread
needle, foam sponges, scissors
access to a sewing machine

Centering an image in your project, regardless of size, ensures a strong focal point as shown here. Refer to page 38 for stamping on fabric before beginning. Sew a ⅛" hem all the way around the white fabric. Stamp a pink Bunny in the center. Use the paintbrush to paint a green scalloped border along the edges. Let dry. Cut the lavender fabric into two 10" squares. Sew the Bunny square to the center of one. Sew a button to each corner. Sew the other buttons to the pillow as shown. Lay the two lavender squares right sides together and sew around them leaving a 3" opening. Turn right side out, stuff and sew the opening closed. For an adorable room deodorizer, sprinkle the fiberfill with baby powder or your favorite scent before stuffing the pillow!

Baby Photo Album

Baby Shoes stamp, brown dye-based ink
white cardstock, tacky glue, scissors
5"x7" olive mini photo album with a gold satin ribbon tie

Even tiny images, when centered, provide a great focal point. The wide border around it helps attract the eye. Stamp the Baby Shoes image onto the card-stock and cut to a 3" square. Glue inside the cover so the image shows through the window.

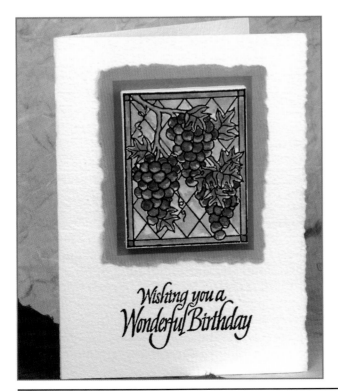

Stained Glass Grapes Card

stamps: "…Wonderful Birthday", Stained Glass Grapes
black pigment ink, clear embossing powder, heat tool
7"x10" ivory watercolor paper
ivory cardstock, 2⅜"x3⅛" piece of foam board
solid color papers: purple, tan
watercolors: yellow, purple, blue, green, tan
#0 round paintbrush, X-acto® knife, tacky glue, scissors

Create a focal point that literally stands out with foam board! Fold the watercolor paper into a card (see page 41) and tear the right edge of the front flap. Stamp and emboss (see page 28) the Grapes image on the cardstock. Paint it, glue it to foam board and cut out with the knife. Mat it on purple then mat again on tan, tearing around the edges. Glue the matted image to the card front. Stamp and emboss the greeting below it.

Mini Shopping Bag Tags

stamps: Floral Beehive, Watering Can Bees
black pigment ink, clear embossing powder, heat tool
ivory cardstock, kraft paper
watercolors: maroon, orange, yellow, brown, tan, green, purple,
* blue, pink*
16" of 1/16" wide brown kraft paper ribbon
#0 round paintbrush, pencil, tacky glue, black fine-tip pen
pinking patterned scissors, straight edged scissors, tracing paper

Stamp and emboss (see page 28) each image onto card-stock. Cut around the upper stamp area leaving a 1½" space below as shown under the Watering Can Bees. Write a message in the area with the pen. Color in the images. Trace the pattern on page 140 and cut out two mini bags. Trim the top edges with patterned scissors. Fold and glue as indicated. Use the pen to write "Bee Happy!" on one, "Just Bee Cuz" on the other and draw a frame. Cut four 4" lengths of ribbon and glue inside each bag edge for handles. Slip the images into the bags.

Rustic Bee Boxes

stamps: Flying Bee, Bee with Hearts
black pigment ink, clear embossing powder, heat tool
papier maché boxes with rusted tin lids: 2⅜"x1½" square,
* 2¼"x1½" round*
acrylic paints: red, yellow
#0 liner paintbrush, matte-acrylic spray sealer, long tongs

Center an image on the box lid to create a strong focal point! Remove the lid from each box. Seal each lid. Stamp one image on each lid. Hold the lid with tongs and emboss (see page 28). Let them cool before handling. Paint the images with the acrylic paints. Let dry and seal.

Sunflower Pot

Woodcut Sunflower stamp
black waterproof ink
ivory paper
6" wide terra cotta pot
olive green acrylic paint
watercolors: yellow, green, peach
paintbrushes: #3 round, 1" wide flat
pinking patterned scissors, decoupage glue

Large images command attention and easily create the focal point of any project. Seal the pot with decoupage glue and let dry. Paint the outside of the pot green as shown. Let dry. Stamp the image onto the ivory paper, color it and trim to 2¾"x4" with patterned scissors. Decoupage (see page 34) the image to the pot. Let dry. Use a plastic liner in the pot if you intend to grow a plant in it.

Balsa Angel Ornament Gift Bag

Sarah Angel stamp
black crafter's ink, 3½"x4" piece of balsa wood
6½" square of burlap, 4½" square of red checked fabric
red checked kraft gift bag, denim patterned Paper Pizazz™
tissue paper: red checked, slate blue
acrylic paints: metallic gold, green, maroon, blue,
    red, yellow, tan
eight ⅜"-⅝" wide assorted buttons
three 15" lengths of natural raffia
#2 round paintbrush, black fine-tip pen
10" of 22-gauge wire, foam tape, X-acto® knife
straightened paper clip, tacky glue
deckle patterned scissors, straight edged scissors

The unique stamping surface of balsa wood creates the focal point in this collage. Stamp the Sarah Angel image onto the wood and paint. Let dry. Use the pen to draw her eyes and smile. Use the knife to cut out the image. Push a paper clip end through each wing tip to make a hole. Coil the wire around the paintbrush handle, remove it and thread one wire end through each hole. Twist the ends to secure. Handle the raffia as one and tie a shoestring bow (see page 41) with 1½" loops and 3" tails then use your fingernails to shred them. Use patterned scissors to cut a 5" square of denim Paper Pizazz™. Collage (see page 35) the elements to the bag front. Lightly adhere the angel in the center with a ½" piece of foam tape so it may be removed and used as an ornament. Insert the tissue paper into the bag.

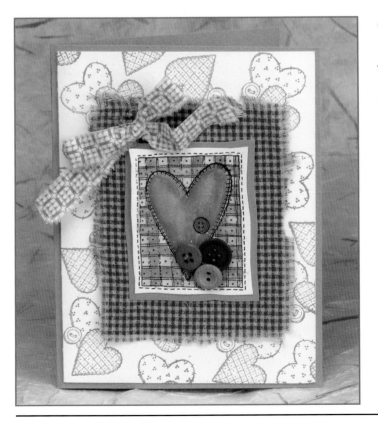

Country Heart Card

stamps: Heart & Button Patch, Heart Cluster
black waterproof ink, slate blue dye-based ink
clear embossing powder, heat tool
cardstock: ivory, blue
watercolors: red, dark blue, light blue
3½"x4½" piece of red checked fabric
9" of ½" wide blue calico fabric
three ½"-⅝" wide buttons
#2 round liner paintbrush, scissors, tacky glue

Showcase one stamped image with interesting mats and lots of color! To make the card, cut a 9½"x6" piece of blue cardstock and fold it (see page 41). Randomly stamp blue Heart Cluster images on ivory cardstock and cut it to 4½"x5¾". Glue to the card front. Stamp and emboss (see page 28) a Heart and Button Patch image on ivory cardstock. Color it in and cut out. Mat it on blue, then glue it to the red checked fabric. Glue this piece to the card front. Tie the calico fabric into a shoestring bow with 1" loops and 2" tails. Glue this, and the buttons to the card front as shown.

Primitive Sun Candle

Primitive Sun stamp
acrylic paints: orange, rust
2¾"x4"x3¾" yellow pillar candle
water-based sealer, embossing heat tool, foam sponges
paintbrushes: #2 round, ½" wide flat

Images impressed on candles will always draw lots of attention! Coat the entire candle surface with sealer and let dry. Apply orange and rust paint to the stamp. Holding the heat tool several inches away, heat (don't melt!) one side of the candle to soften the wax. Immediately press the stamp into the wax. Lift the stamp carefully. Repeat on each candle side. Touch up the paint as needed with the small brush.

Bee Pillow

Bee stamp, black crafter's ink
two 6" square white doilies
fabric markers: yellow, gray
1 yard of ¼" wide black checked ribbon, scissors
1 oz. of polyester fiberfill, fabric glue, needle, thread

Frame a stamped image with ribbon to create a focal point! Refer to page 38 for stamping on fabric before beginning. Stamp the Bee image on one doily center and color it in. Lay the doilies wrong sides together and sew three sides closed 1" in from the edges. Stuff with fiberfill and sew closed. Cut the ribbon into four 6" lengths. Glue each ribbon strip over the stitching to frame the bee image as shown. Use the remaining ribbon to tie a shoestring bow (see page 41) with ¾" loops and 1¼" tails. Glue the bow at one corner.

Wooden Rose Box

stamps: Rose, "Forget me not…"
clear embossing ink, gold embossing powder, heat tool
6½"x3⅛"x5" unfinished wood box with hinged lid
acrylic paints: ivory, gold, pink, green
paintbrushes: ½" wide flat, #4 round
water-based sealer, sandpaper, soft cloth, Post-it® notes

The large painted image on the box top is clearly the focal point of this project. Prepare the wood (see page 36). Paint the box ivory. Let dry. Paint the box lid sides gold and let dry. With the lid open, randomly stamp and emboss (see page 28) portions of the Rose image on the box sides. Stamp and emboss one whole Rose image on the lid center. Mask it (see page 29) then repeatedly stamp and emboss the word image around the image on the lid. Paint the roses and let dry. Mix one part pink paint with one part water and paint the pink wash around the images on the box sides. Let dry then seal.

Magnolia Plate

Magnolia stamp
brown crafter's ink, 9½" octagon unfinished wood plate
colored oil pencils: pink, dark pink, green, dark green
metal ruler, pencil, matte-finish wood sealer
½" wide flat paintbrush, sandpaper, soft cloth
woodburning tool, heavy gloves

A unique technique like woodburning draws even more attention to the focal point image. While the plaid border earns attention, the darker colors used in the image bring it to the forefront. Prepare the wood (see page 36). Stamp the image in the plate center. Use the ruler and pencil to lightly draw plaid lines 1¼" apart around the rim. Follow the manufacturer's directions to use the woodburning tool and go over the image outline and detail lines, plus the drawn plaid lines. Wear heavy gloves and use the metal ruler as a guide (which will get hot!) to help burn perfectly straight lines. Use the oil pencils to color in the image and plaid design. Seal the plate, let dry and seal again.

Birthday Plate

stamps: "Make a Wish", Swirl "Happy Birthday"
black waterproof ink, 8" round glass plate
solid color papers: white, green, black
watercolors: yellow, pink, blue, green
#2 round paintbrush
decoupage glue, scissors, X-acto® knife

Center the most important image of your project to create a focal point—surround it with secondary images as shown here. Cut an 8" round white piece of paper. Stamp the "Make a Wish" image in the center and color it in. **To cut the ½" wide green bands:** cut an 8" wide circle from green paper and use the knife to remove a 7½" wide circle from the center leaving a ½" wide 8" band. Cut 3½" wide circle from the 7½" circle and remove a 3" circle from its center leaving a ½" wide 3" band. Glue the 8" band to the white circle edge and the 3" green band to circle the stamped image. Cut many ½" black squares and glue to the green bands to make a checkered pattern. Repeatedly stamp the "Happy Birthday" image between the two green bands and color them in. Decoupage (see page 34) the circle center to the plate bottom. Apply glue to the plate, cut three slits towards the plate center and wrap the circle up around the plate sides. Trim the edges if necessary. This plate is designed to be used carefully. To clean it, wipe the front surface with a damp cloth. Do not immerse the plate in water.

Alphabet Stamps

This chapter shows how to design great projects using alphabet stamps. Each alphabet stamp consists of an individual letter die on a wood or foam handle. The wide variety of letter styles enables you to create any look to fit any occasion. The two examples—from silly to sophisticated—shown on page 87 illustrate this. The terrific ideas shown in this chapter will help you create lots of different things with alphabet stamps.

Create a personal place to keep treasures with the box on page 84. Or teach a child phonics with the baby blocks shown on page 85. The chunky blocks at the bottom of the same page make an adorable decorative addition to any baby's book shelf!

Letter stamps help you express an emotion, welcome a new friend or invite old ones over as shown with the diverse cards on page 89. Stamp an inspirational message as was done on the frame shown on page 86. Use alphabet stamps to design an elaborate puzzle (like the gift wrap on page 88), or a simple magazine rack (see page 86).

Alphabet stamps look great alone like on the alphabead necklaces and bracelets shown on page 85. They're also fun to collage with images and bits of paper as shown on the matchbox greetings on page 88.

The best part about alphabet stamps is that the individual letters give you the freedom to stamp any name, place or phrase you'd like—they're the perfect way to truly personalize your projects!

This chapter's background paper is from Paper Pizazz™ Handmade Papers.

Keepsake Box

stamps: Pattern Alphabet, Accent Swirl, Accent Heart
stamping paints: black, red
10½"x5"x7" unfinished wood box with sliding lid
acrylic paints: pink, purple, yellow, blue, dark blue, sage green
Paper Pizazz™ patterned papers: purple chalky, black & white checked
solid color papers: red, yellow, sage green, purple, blue
paintbrushes: 1" wide flat, #3 round
foam sponges
decoupage glue
water-based sealer
sandpaper, soft cloth
tracing paper, pencil, ruler, scissors

Prepare the wood (see page 36). Lightly pencil two rows of four 2½" squares on the box front and back, and two rows of three 2½" squares on each box side. Paint each square as shown and let dry. Paint the box lid pink and the rim blue. Stamp red Heart and black Swirl images on the box sides. Trace the pattern on page 142 and paint a yellow flower with a red center on each side. Cut and decoupage (see page 34) six ½"x3" black & white checked Paper Pizazz™ strips on the box sides. Cut ½" wide strips of purple chalky Paper Pizazz™ and decoupage them to border the lid as shown. Cut ¾" wide black & white checked Paper Pizazz™ squares to cover the border corners. Stamp black letters to spell "MY STUFF" on the solid color papers. Tear each letter to a 1½"x1¾" rectangle. Decoupage the letters to the box lid. Finish the lid with two stamped red Hearts. Use the black paint to paint ½" wide stripes on the purple paper border.

Stick Dot Frame & Bookmark

Upper Case Dot ABC Kit, black dye-based ink
white gloss-coated cardstock, 2¼"x6" white gloss-coated bookmark
brush markers: blue, red, orange, green, bright pink
8 assorted ½"-⅝" wide colored buttons, 6" long red tassel
black fine-tip pen, ruler, foam sponges, Post-it® notes
X-acto® knife, scissors, tacky glue, tracing paper, pencil

For the frame: From the cardstock cut two 5½" squares. Cut a 3" square from the center of one. Mask (see page 29) the frame sides. Sponge (see page 32) each corner red. When dry, mask each and sponge the frame sides using the colors shown. Stamp the photo friends' names in black ink then glue buttons to each corner as shown. Glue the frame to a 5½" cardstock square on three sides leaving the top open to slip in a photo. Trace the pattern on page 141 and cut a support and glue it to the frame back.

For the bookmark: Mask the center 1¼"x5" area and each corner of the bookmark. Sponge the exposed area orange, let dry and mask them. Remove the corner masks and sponge them red. Let dry. Mask the border, remove the center masks and sponge four 1¼" squares as shown. Stamp "READ" as shown. Use the pen to draw dots in the orange areas.

Alphabeads Jewelry

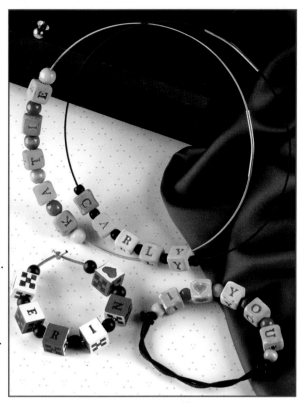

stamp Peg Sets: Antique ABC's, Petite Basic Shapes
crafter's ink: red, black
½" square wood beads (we used 6), air-dry modeling clay
assorted colored round wood beads: 6mm, 8mm, 10mm
brush markers: pink, red, purple, blue, green, orange, lime, yellow
acrylic paints: white, red
15" black cording, 10" gold elastic cording, necklace wires: black, gold
16-gauge wire, water-based sealer, sandpaper, soft cloth
¼" wide flat paintbrush, ruler

For the wood alphabeads: Prepare the wood (see page 36). Paint each bead white, let dry and paint some sides red as shown. Let dry. Stamp contrasting black or red Heart and Checkerboard images onto the beads. Stamp a letter on each bead to spell a name.

For the clay alphabeads: Use your fingers to shape a piece of clay into a ⅜" square. To bore a hole through the bead, push the wire halfway through one bead side then through the other side to meet the first hole inside (this prevents "blow out" on one side). Let the beads harden overnight. Stamp a letter or basic shape on each square side. Color each square a different color with the markers. String the beads onto the necklace wire or cording, separating each alphabead with a round bead and knot.

Chunky Blocks

Decorative stamps: Alphabet Kit, Airplane, Apple, Car, Small Butterfly, Accent Teddy Bear, Accent Crown, Checkerboard
acrylic paints: red, blue, yellow, brown, green, black, gold
three 3" unfinished wood blocks
toothbrush, foam sponges, soft cloth, sandpaper
non-toxic water-based sealer, ½" wide flat paintbrush

To stamp a multi-colored image, use sponges to apply paint to the appropriate portion of the image. Prepare the wood (see page 36). **For the "B" block:** Paint it yellow and stamp red Checkerboards on the top and bottom. Stamp a blue "B" on two sides. Stamp a Bear and Butterfly on the remaining sides. Repeat for the other blocks using the remaining stamps. Notice how the larger images curve around the corner. To spatter each block, dip a damp toothbrush into black paint and pull your thumb across the bristles. Let dry. Use sandpaper to rub the corners smooth. Seal.

Baby Blocks

Stamp & Learn ABC Kit
black crafter's ink
five 1½" unfinished wood blocks
acrylic paints: lavender, green, red, orange, dark blue, yellow, maroon, ivory
watercolors: red, blue, green, brown, yellow, orange, gray
¼" wide paintbrush, soft cloth
non-toxic water-based sealer
sandpaper

These alphabet learning blocks are a great tool for parents and children to play with together. Prepare the wood (see page 36). Paint each block ivory. Let dry. Stamp an upper and lower case letter and coordinating image on opposite block sides. Stamp two letters per block. Paint the other sides a solid color and a ⅛" border around each letter and image. Color each image with the pencils. Sand the edges then seal.

Wood Alpha Frame

*stamp Peg Sets: Monogram ABC's, Antique
    Lower Case ABC's, Antique ABC's
Alphabet Sets: Large Monogram Collection,
    Uppercase, Lowercase
stamps: Versailles Desk Set, Accent Fleur de
    Lis Decorative
black crafter's ink, gold leafing kit
9"x7" unfinished wood frame with a
    5½"x3½" opening
acrylic paints: gold, olive green
1" wide flat paintbrush, paper towels
photograph, water-based sealer
sandpaper, soft cloth, tape*

Prepare the wood (see page 36). Paint
the frame green and let dry. Dip the
brush in gold paint then blot on paper
towels until the brush is almost dry.
Brush gold streaks onto the frame and
around the opening. Use the variety of
Alphabet stamps to stamp "Trust in
Yourself," "Dream," "Live, laugh,
Love" and "Believe." Stamp the alphabet in the lower left corner and ABC above the
opening. Follow the manufacturer's directions to gold leaf small, medium and large fleur de
lis images among the alphabet stamps as shown. Let dry then seal. Tape the photo to the
frame back so it shows through the opening.

Magazine Rack

*Decorative stamp Alphabet Kit
acrylic paints: light and medium blue
golden yellow stamping paint
24"x13"x4½" unfinished wood
    magazine rack
water-based sealer, sandpaper
tracing paper, ruler, pencil
foam sponges, soft cloth
paintbrushes: ½" wide flat,
    1" wide flat*

Prepare the wood (see
page 36). Paint the front
and back of the rack light
blue. Paint the side
boards medium blue.
Paint three ¾" squares on
the front board sides as shown.
Trace the pattern on page 142, cut it out and
use it to draw the diamond pattern onto the back board.
Paint the diamond shapes medium blue. Paint a ½" yellow square to
overlap the diamond points as shown. Stamp yellow letters to write
"MAGAZINES" on the rack front. Let dry and seal.

"Best Friends" Scrapbook

Pattern Alphabet Kit
dye-based inks: red, black
two 10"x8" pieces of red mat board
1¾"x8" black corrugated cardboard
4 gold grommets & tool, filler paper
24" of ¼" wide red checked ribbon

For the cover: stamp black letters to read "Best Friends" as shown on one red mat board piece. Stamp red swirls to fill the empty spaces.

For the journal: Lay the mat boards together red sides out and insert the filler paper. Glue the corrugated strip along the left binding side. Follow the manufacturer's instructions to insert the grommets 5" apart along the binding length. Thread the ribbon through back to front and tie a shoestring bow (see page 41) with 2" loops and 4" tails.

Monogram Photo Holder

Illuminated Initial stamp (we used the letter "D")
clear embossing ink, heat tool
gold embossing powder
2½" square of brass metal sheeting
black photo album with ribbon tie
tacky glue

Stamp and emboss (see page 28) the initial onto the metal sheeting. Use care when handling as the metal will get very hot. Glue the sheeting inside the front cover so the letter shows through the window in the photo holder.

Crossword Card & Gift Wrap

Uppercase and Antique ABC Peg Sets,
Checkerboard stamp
black dye-based and pigment inks, heat tool
clear embossing powder, red brush marker
kraft paper, 4¾" square white card
red cardstock
½" wide black & white checked ribbon
black fine-tip pen, glue, scissors, ruler

For the card: Using pigment ink, stamp and emboss (see page 28) a Checkerboard pattern on a 4¾" square of kraft paper. Glue it to the card front. Cut a 3⅛" square of red cardstock. Use the ruler and pen to draw horizontal and vertical lines every ¼" to create 121 squares. Stamp an Antique ABC letter in each square. Stamp out "I Heard It's Your Birthday Today" on kraft paper. Cut each letter to ¼" squares and glue them to the red kraft paper as shown.

For the gift wrap: Cut enough kraft paper to cover the gift. Stamp the words "Happy Birthday [Name]" in the center. Use the marker to circle and color the words as shown. Randomly stamp letters in straight lines to cover the paper. Wrap the gift then tie the ribbon around it in a shoestring bow (see page 41).

Matchbox Greetings

stamps: Antique ABC's Peg Set, Antique Lowercase Peg Set,
Toy Ball Man, Toy Dog, Penguin Pull Toy, Toy Rabbit,
Rocking Horse, Heart, Heart on Fire, Swirl Heart,
Checkerboard Heart, Swirl Heart Open, Heart &
Arrows, Large Swirl Heart
red dye-based ink, black waterproof ink
clear embossing ink, gold embossing powder, heat tool
white cardstock, white paper
Paper Pizazz™ patterned papers: red checked, burgundy
striped, blue paisley, purple paisley, lines & dots on blue,
dots on red, pink hearts on purple, burgundy suede,
gold metallic
watercolors: black, red, green, yellow, purple, brown, gray
paintbrushes: #0 round, #2 round
scissors, ruler, glue, tracing paper, pencil

Trace the pattern on page 140 and cut the matchbox tray from the cardstock. To make the cover, cut a 2½"x5½" cardstock strip. Tear pieces of Paper Pizazz™ to glue on. Stamp a message and image as shown. Wrap the cover around the tray and glue to secure. Cut a 2¼" tall strip of white paper—it can be as long as you'd like! Stamp images and messages as shown here. Use a variety of letters for interest. Emboss (see page 28) some images. Color each image with watercolors. Tear Paper Pizazz™ pieces and glue around the images and messages. Let dry. Fan fold your greeting strip every 1⅝" so it will fit in the matchbox. Put the greeting in the tray and slip it into the cover.

Alphabet Cards

*stamps: Antique ABC's Peg Set, Antique Lower case ABC's
    Peg Set, Alphabet Decorative Set, Baby Border, Baby
    Bottle, Garden Hat, Simple Daisy Decorative, Open Swirl
inks: clear embossing & pen, black & pink waterproof
stamping paints: gold, silver
gold embossing powder, heat tool
cardstock: ivory, pale pink, red, 4"x5¼" white card
watercolors: pink, yellow, green, tan
12" of 1" wide gold mesh ribbon, ⅛" hole punch
scissors, foam mounting tape, #0 round paintbrush
ruler, tacky glue, foam sponges*

For the Love card: Stamp a gold "L" and "E", a
silver "V" and two silver Daisies with gold centers
onto red cardstock. Stamp and emboss (see page 28)
the open swirl image on the "L" and "E". Cut each
image out. Fold a 10"x6¾" piece of red cardstock to
make a card. Adhere the letters and Daisies to the
card front as show with foam mounting tape. Use
the ruler and embossing pen to emboss a gold border
at the card top and bottom, and to emboss small dots
in the daisy center.

For the Garden Invitation: Stamp a black Hat
image on the ivory cardstock, paint it and cut it to
3¼"x3¾". Mat (see page 41) it on a 4"x4½" piece of
pale pink. Cut a 4"x5" piece of ivory and stamp a
pink "Garden Party" at the bottom. Cut a 4"x5¼"
pale pink piece of cardstock. Layer them as shown,
punch two holes ½" apart and ¾" from the top
and thread the ribbon through back to front. Tie a
shoestring bow with 1½" loops and 2½" tails.

For the baby announcement: Cut a 1½" square
window in the center of the white note card. Use the
embossing pen and ruler to draw a line to frame it,
then another ⅛" away. Draw small squares between
the two lines to make the checkerboard frame and
emboss it. Stamp and emboss "Look Who's Here"
below the window. Mask (see page 29) the window
border and message. Repeatedly stamp and emboss
isolated Baby Border and Baby Bottle images on the
card. Cut a photo to 2"x2" and glue it inside the
front card flap so it shows through the window.

Frame Stamps

Frame stamps imprint the image of a frame and include elements like words and designs. They vary from small to quite large and can be used to frame photos and lots more! The finishing touch—what's framed inside—is up to you!

Stamp a frame on paper, remove the center and place it over a photo as the projects on page 96 show. Or stamp the frame directly on the surface, cut your photo to fit and glue it on top of the frame opening as shown in the projects on page 94.

There's a frame stamp that will compliment any photo you have! Frame your pet in paw prints, as shown on page 96. Or frame your family members with written sentiments of endearment as shown on page 93.

Although photographs are the most common things to be framed, frames don't have to be filled only with them! Fill a frame with a charm as shown on page 92, or something even more unusual—clay buttons made with rubber stamps (shown at the top of page 95)!

Besides stamping a frame on paper, this chapter includes frame stamps on projects such as refrigerator magnets (page 95), a wood triptych (page 94), and a jewelry box (page 92)! It's easy to see how versatile and creatively useful frame stamps really are!

This chapter's background paper is from Paper Pizazz™ Handmade Papers.

Jewelry Box & Mini Frames

stamps: Wrought Iron Frame,
*   Tribal Frame, Checkerboard,*
*   Accent Scroll Decorative*
clear embossing ink, heat tool
gold embossing powder
3¼"x1⅞"x3¼" unfinished wood
*   box with gold clasp*
black mat board, black cardstock
stamping paints: black, gold
charms: 1⅛" tall gold ballerina,
*   ½" wide gold flower*
photograph, sandpaper, soft cloth
¼" wide paintbrush, tacky glue
water-based sealer, X-acto® knife
tracing paper, pencil, scissors

For the box: Remove the clasp from the box. Prepare the wood (see page 36). Paint the box black; let dry. Paint the lid sides gold. Paint a gold ⅜" wide border around the lid top; let dry. Stamp and emboss (see page 28) the Wrought Iron image on the lid top center. Stamp a black Checkerboard image around the lid sides. Use the gold paint to stamp the Accent Scroll image around the box sides. Let dry. Seal the box and glue the ballerina charm in the frame center. Replace the clasp.

For the frames: Cut two 2¼" black mat board squares; paint them gold. Trace the pattern on page 141 and cut frame supports from mat board. Glue one to the back of each. Stamp and emboss each Frame image onto black cardstock. Trim each to a 1⅞" square. Glue the flower charm in the center of the Tribal image and glue to one frame. Use the knife to cut out the center of the Wrought Iron image, glue it over the photo and glue to the other frame.

Frame Collage Card

"How do I love thee…" stamp
clear embossing ink and pen, gold embossing powder
4½"x6" piece of purple handmade paper
4¼"x5½" piece of ivory parchment paper
10"x6½" piece of natural cardstock
gold tiles patterned Paper Pizazz™
1¼" long brass heart charm
9" of ⅛" wide gold mesh ribbon
spray adhesive, tacky glue, X-acto® knife, heat tool

Refer to page 41 to fold the cardstock into a card. Cover the card with the gold tiles Paper Pizazz™. Stamp the frame onto the parchment paper and emboss (see page 28). Tear around the stamped words and use the embossing pen and powder to emboss the edges. Use the knife to cut out the frame center. Thread the ribbon through the charm eye and tie a shoestring bow with 1" loops and 2" tails. Combine the elements using collage techniques (see page 35) to make this very romantic card.

Gold tiles paper from Paper Pizazz™ book *Embossed Papers,* HOTP 3052

A Framed Friend

Friendship Frame stamp
clear embossing ink, gold embossing powder, heat tool
burgundy crushed suede patterned Paper Pizazz™
5"x7" gold frame, photograph, scissors, tacky glue

Cut the Paper Pizazz™ to fit inside the frame. Stamp and emboss (see page 28) the Friendship Frame image in the center of the paper. Cut the photo to fit and glue inside the center opening. Remove the frame back, put the paper in and replace the frame back.

Family Photo Album

stamps: Family Frame, "May my heart…"
clear embossing ink, gold embossing powder, heat tool
12"x12" unfinished wood post-bound album
color copied black and white photographs
sandpaper, soft cloth, antique medium, old cloth
decoupage glue, ½" wide paintbrush, scissors

Disassemble the album. Prepare the wood (see page 36). Follow the manufacturer's instructions to antique the cover pieces. Stamp and emboss (see page 28) the Family Frame image on the cover center and the "May my heart…" image along the spine front. Tear the photo edges and decoupage (see page 34) them to the cover. Cut one photo to fit the Family Frame center and glue in place. Reassemble the album.

Wedding Album

stamps: Romantic Rose Large Bouquet, Romantic Roses Heart Frame
embossing powders: silver, clear; white pigment ink, clear embossing pen
8½"x10" journal with white handmade paper cover
4"x5¼" piece of mauve paper, 3¾"x5" piece of vellum Paper Pizazz™
silver metallic Paper Pizazz™: 4½"x5¾" piece, 5"x10" strip
brush markers: pink, green
white photo corners, 1" wide silver heart charm
18" of 1" wide silver mesh ribbon
deckle patterned scissors, straight edged scissors, tacky glue, heat tool

Use the patterned scissors to trim the long edges of the silver Paper Pizazz™ strip. Repeatedly stamp and emboss (see page 28) a white Bouquet image on it. Open the book, lay the spine in the strip center and glue to secure. Draw around the vellum Paper Pizazz™ edges with the embossing pen and emboss with silver powder. Stamp and emboss a white Heart Frame in the center. Color the image on the back. Trim the mauve and silver papers with patterned scissors. Affix the mauve paper to the silver Paper Pizazz™ piece with photo corners. Glue the vellum to the mauve paper. Trim each ribbon edge diagonally, fold it in half and glue the matted frame piece 1" below the fold to the journal cover center. Fold the ribbon over the frame and glue the charm to the ribbon center.

Hanging Oval Frames

Antique Oval Frame stamp
pigment inks: red, yellow, purple, blue
clear embossing ink, heat tool
white gloss-coated cardstock
1⅔ yards of 1" wide polka dot ribbon
4 photographs
scissors, tacky glue

Use the ribbon to tie a shoestring bow (see page 41) with 2" loops and 26" tails. Trim each tail diagonally. Stamp and emboss (see page 28) the Oval Frame onto the cardstock once in each color. Cut out. Glue each oval spaced 1" apart along the ribbon tails as shown. Cut each photo to fit and glue inside the frames.

Sisters Triptych

stamps: Sisters Frame, Flowers Desk set; black pigment ink, clear embossing powder
11"x10" unfinished wood triptych, acrylic paints: white, yellow, fuchsia, green, black
sandpaper, soft cloth, tacky glue, water-based sealer, scissors, heat tool
paintbrushes: 1" wide, ¼" wide, #0 round

Prepare the wood (see page 36). Paint the triptych white; let dry. Apply tape strips ¼" apart along the edges. Paint black between the tapes. Remove and let dry. Stamp and emboss (see page 28) the Sisters Frame in the triptych center. Paint ¼" wide yellow stripes 1" apart on the triptych front. Randomly stamp and emboss the Rosebud image in the empty spaces. Paint each image. Let dry then seal.

Rosebud Keepsake Box

Decorative stamps: Polka Dot Frame, Rose Stem
stamping paints: yellow, fuchsia, green, white
6¾"x3⅛"x6¾" papier mâché box, white matte-coated sticker paper
9" of ⅜" wide fuchsia with white dots grosgrain ribbon, tacky glue
photograph, scissors, new pencil with eraser, foam sponges

Isolate (see page 29) the stamp portions to print only fuchsia bud images on the box lid, green leaves on each bud side, and the full Rose Stem image along the box sides. Re-apply paint for each impression. Paint the lid sides yellow; let dry. Dip the pencil eraser in white paint and lightly touch it to the lid sides to make dots. Apply yellow paint to the Polka Dot Frame stamp and press onto the sticker paper; cut out and affix to the box lid. Tie the ribbon into a shoestring bow (see page 41) with 2" loops and 1½" tails and glue as shown. Cut the photo to fit and glue inside the frame.

Buttons

stamps: Lamb, Heart, Frog, Rabbit, Bear,
Checkerboard Frame, Antique ABC Peg Set
pigment inks: green, pink, red, blue
black crafter's ink, clear embossing powder
heat tool, air dry clay
cardstock: five 4"x5" pieces of white,
five 4¼"x5¼ pieces of black
acrylic paints: red, black, brown, yellow, green,
pink, white, peach, blue
#0 paintbrush, scissors, X-acto® knife, toothpick
sewing needle & black thread, rolling pin or 1" dowel
tacky glue, emery board or sandpaper, acrylic sealer

Roll the clay to ⅛" thick. Use crafter's ink to stamp each image twice onto the clay. Use the knife to cut around each image. Use the toothpick to poke two button holes into each image center. Let dry overnight. Rub the edges smooth with sandpaper. Paint as shown. Follow the manufacturer's instructions to apply two coats of sealer. Stamp and emboss (see page 28) the Checkerboard Frames onto white cardstock in the colors shown. Use the letters to stamp "BUTTONS" above each. Sew two buttons to each frame center with the needle and thread. Glue the edges of each frame to a piece of black cardstock. Finished buttons are not washable.

Photo Magnets

frame stamps: Sports, Newsworthy, Birthday Cake, Camera,
"Wanted" Poster
brush markers: red, purple, teal, blue, yellow, tan, brown,
pink, lavender
white gloss-coated paper magnetic sheets
scissors, photographs, black fine-tip permanent-ink pen

Apply the marker colors to the stamps. Stamp each frame image onto the white side of the magnetic sheets. Cut around the images. Cut photos to fit and glue inside the frames. Use the pen to personalize the magnets.

Accordion Frame Folder

stamps: Polka Dot Frame, Checkerboard Frame,
Posh Creative Corner Rubber Stamp Kit
pigment inks: purple, green, pink, blue, yellow
clear embossing powder, heat tool
matte-coated sticker paper, 21⅛"x5¼" white cardstock
Paper Pizazz™ patterned papers: green plaid, pink & blue
plaid, pink with white stitching, blue with pink hearts
4 photographs, X-acto® knife, tacky glue, scissors

Fold the cardstock accordion style every 5¼". Cut the Paper Pizazz™ sheets to fit and glue one onto each square. Stamp and emboss (see page 28) the Frame and Corner stamps onto sticker paper, cut out and remove the frame centers. Cut each photo slightly smaller than the frame. Remove the frame backing and affix a photo to each square with the sticker frame. Embellish the first and third frames with the corner stamps as shown.

Vacation Frames

Frame stamps: Postcard, Fishing, Paradise; black waterproof ink
three 4"x5½" pieces of ivory cardstock
black mat board pieces: three 4½"x5¾", three 2½"x5"
background papers: 6"x4¾" brown wavy corrugated, 6"x4½" copper
  handmade, 6¼"x4¾" rust & gray handmade, 5¾"x4⅜" green
colored pencils: blue, red, yellow, green, gold, orange, brown
photographs, tracing paper, pencil, X-acto® knife, tacky glue
deckle patterned scissors, straight edged scissors

Stamp each frame image onto ivory cardstock, color the images and cut out the centers. Tear the edges of the handmade papers. Trim the edges of the Fishing Frame and green paper with patterned scissors. Glue the green to the gray handmade piece. Glue three sides of each Frame to the background papers

as shown, leaving the tops open to slip in a photo. Glue each to a large black mat board piece. Trace the frame support pattern on page 141, cut from mat board and affix to each frame back.

Scrapbooking Pet Pages

stamps: Dog Frame, Kitty Frame, Paw Print, Thomas Cat, Duffy Kitty,
  Fred Dog, Happy Puppy
black pigment ink, clear embossing powder, heat tool
Paper Pizazz™ patterned papers: barnwood, 12"x12" tri-dots on pink,
  12"x12" circles on red
acid-free solid color papers: olive, purple, ivory, white, red
watercolors: pink, brown, tan, yellow, red, gray
acid-free brush markers: blue, brown, yellow, red
photographs, 3-ring binder, two 12"x12" sheet protectors, scissors
acid-free black fine-tip permanent-ink pen
X-acto® knife, archival quality glue

Stamp and emboss (see page 28) the Frame stamps onto white paper. Remove the centers and color in the images. Color the Frame background or leave it blank. Cut your photos slightly larger than the Frame centers and glue them to the Frame backs so the photo shows through the opening. Then glue them on coordinating papers. Cut the paper with a ⅛" border as shown. Silhouette cut a photo (like the kitten) or mat (see page 41) a photo like on the dog page. Arrange the pieces on ivory paper. Stamp and emboss Paw Prints in the empty areas. For the lower picture on the dog page, stamp two Dog images to overlap where the photo will be. Color them in. Use the knife to cut around part of them then slip the photo behind. For a patterned journal area as on the kitty page, cut a 3⅛"x2¼" rectangle from barnwood paper, cut out the center leaving a ½" border and slip it under a partially cut stamp. Draw a border around the whole page or round the corners. Glue the page to Paper Pizazz™ background paper. Slip it into a sheet protector then into a 3-ring binder.

Calendar Page

stamps: "Twinkle…" Frame, Star, Uppercase Alphabet Set, Number Set
pigment inks: red, black, blue, light blue, yellow
clear embossing powder, heat tool,
blank acid-free calendar, acid-free solid color papers: red, yellow, white
acid-free brush markers: yellow, light blue
straight edged scissors, patterned scissors: ripply, pinking
archival quality glue, 2 photographs
tracing paper, pencil, foam sponges

Sponge a cloud background (see page 33). Use foam sponges to apply black ink to the letters, light blue ink to the stars and yellow ink to the moon portions of the Twinkle Frame stamp. Stamp and emboss (see page 28) two Frame images on white paper; cut each out with pinking scissors. Mat (see page 41) onto solid color paper and trim ⅛" away with ripply scissors. Cut a photo to fit and glue one in each star center. Arrange on the cloud background. Stamp and emboss Star images around the matted photos. Color each blue. Stamp and emboss the month's name and numbers on the calendar page. Stamp and emboss two Stars on each side of the month. Color in yellow.

Quilted Hearts Memory Book

stamps: Heart Frame, Heart & Button Patch, Heart Cluster, Heart String
10"x10" spiral bound memory album with ivory cover
black waterproof ink, #0 round paintbrush
watercolors: green, red, blue, yellow, pink
black fine-tip permanent-ink pen, ruler

Stamp the Heart Frame in the cover center. Use the pen to write "Memories" in the Frame center. Stamp a Heart & Button Patch image ¼" in from each cover corner. Stamp a Heart String image above and below the Heart Frame stamp; stamp two Heart Cluster images to the right and left of the Heart Frame stamp. Color in each image with watercolors. Use the pen to draw patch work, stitch lines, tri-dots and polka dots on the cover as shown.

Christmas Frame Card

Christmas Frame stamp, black pigment ink
clear embossing powder, heat tool, 6¼"x5" red card, white paper
watercolors: green, blue, dark green, red, yellow
Paper Pizazz™ patterned papers: tri-dots on green, burgundy with white stars
½" wide red button, 9" of ½" wide burgundy checked ribbon
photograph, tacky glue, pinking patterned scissors

Stamp and emboss (see page 28) the Frame onto white paper. Color the images as shown. Cut around the outline, mat (see page 41) it on the burgundy with white stars Paper Pizazz™ and trim ¼" larger with pinking scissors. Mat it on the tri-dots Paper Pizazz™ and glue to the card front. Tie the ribbon into a shoestring bow with 1½" loops and tails. Glue it and the button as shown.

Stamping A Scene

Once you learn how to build a scene, a door is opened to a whole world of great stamping designs! The easiest way to get started is with a scenery stamp kit. They include all the images necessary to create beautiful scenery in any of your projects from nature scenes to Halloween scenes to Christmas scenes and more. The best part about scene stamping kits is that the images are designed in perfect proportion to one another.

Scenery stamp kits aren't the only way to build a scene, though. All that's needed are images that relate to one theme. Both broad surface and outline stamps work well, as the projects in this chapter demonstrate! In addition, decorative foam stamps give great results like the Pine Tree, Moose and Cloud images shown on page 100. Outline stamps such as the Camellias and Glazed Pot come together nicely to create a quaint bouquet window card shown on page 101.

Stamping scenes in your projects is easy! Different techniques can be used to create an elaborate illusion of dimension or depth. The birthday bear card employed masking to create the look of a three dimensional living room party while the memory page used sticker paper to overlay images on a scenic background. You'll see both projects on page 103! Adding depth with stamping paint only depends on what color is applied first, as shown at the top of page 100 and on page 102. Foam mounting tape makes a terrific dimensional design accessory as shown in the projects on page 101.

Scenery building invites the viewer to visually walk into your project and have a look around! As this chapter shows, making a scene is easier than you think!

This chapter's background paper is from Paper Pizazz™ Handmade Papers.

Cabin Photo Frame

stamps: Pine Tree Decorative, Moose Decorative, Cloud Decorative, Uppercase Alphabet set
stamping paints: sky blue, dark green, light green, pale gray, dark brown, brown, tan, black
9" square cardboard frame with a 3" opening
black brush marker
1⅓ yard of ½" wide green grosgrain ribbon
foam sponges, scissors, tacky glue

When using paint to stamp a scene, stamp the light colors first to avoid having to mask. Paint the lower frame half tan, rounding the horizon line like a hill. Paint the upper frame half sky blue. Stamp two pale gray clouds in the sky. Stamp black letters to read "AT THE CABIN". Apply brown paint to the moose body and dark brown paint to the antlers and hooves. Stamp two moose in the foreground. Let dry and use the marker to draw their eyes and smiles. Stamp three light green trees with brown trunks around the frame opening. Let dry. Stamp the dark green trees with brown trunks to fill the spaces as shown. Stamp the foreground light green tree in the frame corner as shown. Cut a 12" ribbon length and glue it to line the center frame opening. Use the rest to wrap around the outer frame edges.

Scenic Sunset Card

Stamp A Scene stamp kit
brush markers: orange, pink, yellow, blue, purple, aqua, dark green, green, brown, tan
6"x4½" white gloss-coated card
6⁵⁄₁₆"x4¾" green cardstock
iridescent glitter, tacky glue
Post-it® notes, scissors, foam sponges

Mask (see page 29) a horizon line 1⅝" from the card top. Stamp blue mountains working from left to right across the sky center. Sponge (see page 32) purple below them. Use a purple marker to highlight some peaks as shown. Mask the mountains. Sponge yellow, orange, pink and blue for a sunset. Stamp an orange sun in the center. Remove the masks. Sponge yellow and purple as a sunset reflection in the card center as shown. Sponge blue water for 1⅜" across the card then stamp blue and purple waves. Stamp a hilly shoreline of brown and green. Use different shades of the colors to create more depth. Stamp grass, rocks and trees as shown. Mat (see page 41) it on the cardstock. Spread glue onto the sun and reflection and sprinkle with glitter.

Camellia Window Card

stamps: Camellias, Glazed Pot
brush markers: pink, violet, purple, green, tan
5¼" square white card, white gloss-coated cardstock
purple azaleas patterned Paper Pizazz™, lavender paper
foam mounting tape, scissors, clear acetate
tacky glue, X-acto® knife

Foam mounting tape makes this dimensional window card a cinch to create! Cut a 5¼" square of lavender paper and cut out a 3¼" square from the center. Glue it to the card front. Cut a 5¼" square of cardstock. Glue a 5¼" square of azaleas Paper Pizazz™ to the front and cut out a 3¼" square from the center. Glue a 4" square of acetate to the back. Stamp two Pot images and three flower images onto cardstock. Cut each out. Glue one Pot and Camellia image inside the lavender frame on the card front. Adhere the second Pot and Camellia images over the first using foam mounting tape. Cut the leaves off the third Camellia image and adhere only the blossoms over the second set with foam mounting tape. Cut two 1½"x5¼" cardstock strips. Cover one side with patterned paper and the other with lavender paper. Fan-fold four ⅜" folds lengthwise. Glue the back fold to the card front and the front fold to the window back on each side of the card so that the potted Camellia shows through the window.

top view of card

"Thanks A Bunch" Card

stamps: Design a Flower kit, "Thanks a Bunch"
brush markers: lavender, purple, light blue, yellow, green, light green, burgundy, mauve
4½"x6" white card, white gloss-coated cardstock
gloss-coated sticker paper
pink plaid patterned Paper Pizazz™
iridescent glitter, scissors, tacky glue
foam mounting tape

Use sticker paper to easily layer images without masking or having to worry about ink overlay! Cover the card (see page 41) with pink plaid Paper Pizazz™. Stamp many flower and leaf images onto sticker paper. Cut out and adhere to the card front as shown. Stamp flower images onto the cardstock and cut out. Use foam mounting tape to adhere an entire blossom image (such as the far left flower) or just a portion (as with the lower purple flower center) over it's matching image. Repeat for even more dimension as with the upper right flower center. Stamp the message in the open area at the card top. Apply a dab of glue to the flower centers and sprinkle glitter on them. Let dry.

Bouquet of Flowers

stamps: Anemone Decorative, Daisy Duo Decorative,
   Ivy Decorative, Flowers stamp set, Leaf stamp set,
   Happy Birthday
stamping paints: burgundy, mauve, yellow, green,
   light green, lavender, tan
watercolor paper, white paper
⅞ yard of 1½" wide mauve polka dotted sheer ribbon
wavy edged ruler, #0 round paintbrush
new pencil with eraser, tracing paper
scissors, foam sponges

The color blending technique shown on page 27
helps create beautiful flower blossoms! Stamp
this flower bouquet by stamping the flowers
first, then the foliage. Paint the stems by hand
last. Apply paint to the appropriate portion of
the decorative stamps and stamp each image
within an 8" width onto the watercolor paper.
Stamp "Happy Birthday" at the base. Cut around
the bouquet and sponge burgundy around the
   top edge. Dip the pencil eraser into yellow
      paint and press it in the empty areas to make
      berries. Use the paintbrush to paint stems
      and vines. Let dry. Trace the pattern below.
      Cut it out and use it to cut the bouquet
      holder from white paper. Cut a 1" long slit
      in each side as indicated. Stamp green leaves
      and mauve flowers as shown and fold it
   around the card. Thread the ribbon through the
   slits and tie in a shoestring bow (see page 41) with 2"
loops and 4" tails.

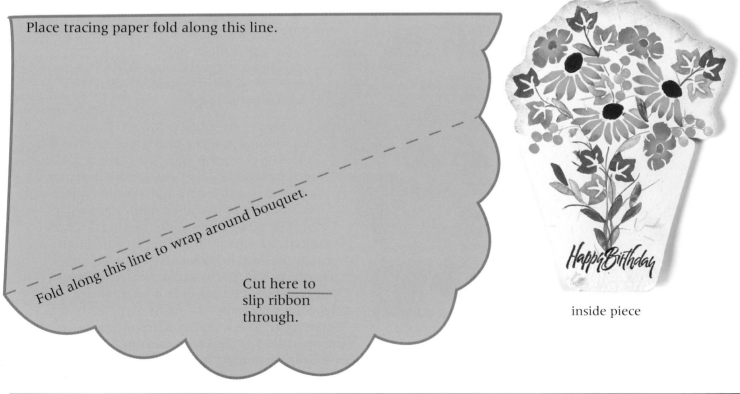

Place tracing paper fold along this line.

Fold along this line to wrap around bouquet.

Cut here to
slip ribbon
through.

inside piece

Off to School Memory Page

stamps: School House, School Bus, ABC Slate, Stamp a Scene kit
black pigment ink, clear embossing powder, heat tool
white sticker paper
acid free solid color papers: white, 3 pieces of red
I Can Draw patterned Paper Pizazz™
brush markers: dark green, green, blue, red, yellow, brown,
   lime, orange, gray
white opaque marker, black acid free permanent-ink pen
foam sponges, scissors, archival quality glue, 2 photographs
sheet protector, 3-ring binder, tracing paper, pencil

Stamp and emboss (see page 28) the School House,
Bus and 5 Slate images onto sticker paper. Color in
each image and cut out. Cut out the center of one
Slate image, adhere it to sticker paper and cut it out
to give it a white background. Use the black pen to
write the year on it. Cut the apples away from the
other four Slate images for photo stickers as shown.
Cut the white paper to 7¼"x8½". Sponge blue clouds
(see page 33) along the upper 3½" and use black to sponge a gray
road curving in from the right as shown. Stamp green long grass images to line
the road and green short grass images to fill the white space. Stamp a tree on the left,
restamping in different shades of green to make lots of leaves. Add the sticker images as shown.
Trim the photos and mat (see page 41) them on red. Glue them as shown adding the apple
stickers. Stamp and emboss a color blended (see page 26) sun at the page top. Mat the page on
red paper, then glue it to the I Can Draw Paper Pizazz™. Cut ⅛" from each edge and glue to the
remaining red sheet. Slip into the sheet protector and then into the 3-ring binder

Birthday Bear Card

Birthday Bear stamp kit, black waterproof ink
watercolors: green, yellow, violet, red, blue, lime,
   purple, orange, turquoise, brown, beige
blue cardstock: 6½"x5", 2"x1½"
red cardstock: 6⅛"x4¾", 1⅞"x1"
ivory cardstock: 5⅞"x9", 1¾"x⅞"
tacky glue, paintbrushes: #0 round, #2 liner
foam mounting tape, pencil, green fine-tip pen

To make a great party room, stamp the images
first, mask them, then paint a background! Refer
to page 41 to make a top-folding card from the
large ivory cardstock. Stamp the Birthday Bear in
the center card front. Stamp a cake and present
on the right. Stamp a present on the left, mask
it (see page 29) and stamp two more in front of
the first. Stamp balloon bouquets as shown and mask all the
images. Use the pencil to draw a table under the cake, a rug under the
bear, horizontal baseboard and chair rail lines behind the bear and vertical
wallpaper lines on the upper wall. Draw floor board lines on the floor. Use
the watercolors to paint the images as shown. Remove the masks. Use the
green pen to draw vines on the wallpaper. Stamp the word image on the
small ivory cardstock and mat it as shown. Adhere it to the card front with
foam mounting tape. Glue the card to red cardstock then onto blue.

Barn Yard Card

Farm Animals stamp kit, black waterproof ink
watercolors: brown, pink, gray, yellow, orange, light
orange, tan
cardstock: 5½"x4½" red, 5½"x9" beige, ivory
brush markers: black, orange
10" length of raffia
paintbrushes: #2 liner, #0 round
X-acto® knife, scissors, glue,

Fold the beige cardstock into a top-folding card (see page 41). Cover with the red cardstock. Trace the framing patterns on page 141 and use them to cut roof and door frame pieces from the ivory card-stock. Glue them as shown. Outline each frame piece in orange marker and make dots for nails as shown. Draw black vertical lines ⅜"-¼" apart outside the door frame and ⅛" apart inside the door frame. Stamp the animals and grass on ivory and color them in. Cut around each. Cut six 2" long raffia pieces and glue above the door. Glue the sitting hen over them. Glue the grass and remaining animals around the barn door. Trim the card top to follow the roof line.

Haunted House Pop-Up Card

stamps: Haunted House, Rest In Peace, "Happy Halloween",
Halloween Stamper Pak, Stamp A Scene kit
pigment inks: black, red, yellow
two 5¼" square white cards, white cardstock
brush markers: yellow, orange, purple, dark blue, light purple,
green, dark green, brown, red
clear embossing powder, heat tool, clear iridescent glitter
glue pen, scissors, X-acto® knife, foam mounting dots
foam sponges, tracing paper, pencil

Stamp and emboss (see page 28) each image on card-stock. Color them in with brush markers and cut them out. Leave a ¼" wide tab along the bottom of the fence and pumpkins. Turn a card to open from the bottom. Sponge purple clouds (see page 33) on the inside top flap and sponge the bottom flap green. Sponge a crooked path of grass and brown rocks up the center bottom of the card to the fold. Use the glue pen to outline the cloud shapes in the sky then sprinkle with glitter. Stamp and emboss black bats as shown. Cut two 2½" long vertical slits ½" apart in the card left and two 1" long vertical slits 2" apart in the card right both beginning ½" above the fold and extending below the fold. Pop these pieces up and glue the skeleton and house to them. Fold the tabs back on the remaining pieces and glue to stand up from the grass. Stamp extra rocks and grass in the empty areas. Stamp and emboss a color blended (see page 26) "Happy Halloween" on card-stock, cut out and adhere to the sky with foam mounting dots. Stamp and emboss a ghost and bat, cut out and adhere with foam mounting dots. Glue the card inside the remaining card. Be careful not to glue the pop-up tabs of the house and skeleton, so that when the card is opened, they pop up!

Happy Harvest Card

Scarecrow with 3 Pumpkins stamp, black pigment ink
clear embossing powder, heat tool
4¾"x6" ivory card, ivory cardstock, yellow paper
Paper Pizazz™ patterned papers: green plaid, grass
watercolors: orange, blue, red, peach, yellow, brown
five 7" strands of raffia
#0 round paintbrush, tacky glue, foam mounting tape
scissors, fine-tip pens: black, brown

Even a single image like this Scarecrow stamp can be used to create a scene! Stamp and emboss (see page 28) a Scarecrow image and two left pumpkin images on the cardstock then cut out. Paint the Scarecrow and pumpkins as shown. Cut the grass Paper Pizazz™ to fit and glue on the card front (see page 41). Cut a 4⅜"x5¾" piece of cardstock, paint it orange and glue to the card. Tear a piece of cardstock to 3¾"x5" and glue to the card. Tear the green plaid Paper Pizazz™ into many ¼"x¾" pieces. Tear the yellow paper into four ¾" long ovals. Draw brown lines for corn nibblets. Glue the corn stalk pieces as shown. Tie two 7" long raffia strands into a shoestring bow. Cut the rest to 1"-3" long pieces and glue to the card front. Adhere the Scarecrow and pumpkins with foam mounting tape. Use the black pen to write "HAPPY HARVEST" on a card scrap and tear around it. Tear another scrap slightly larger, paint orange, and glue the pieces as shown. Draw dashed hill lines under the Scarecrow.

Christmas Window Card

Trim a Home stamp kit, Stamp A Scene kit
black pigment ink, white pigment ink
clear embossing powder, heat tool
4½"x6" white card, white sticker paper
barnwood patterned Cards In Minutes™ card
red with white dots patterned Paper Pizazz™
brush markers: green, dark green, red, gray, pink,
  blue, brown
white Liquid Appliqué™, iridescent glitter
16" of ¼" wide green and blue plaid ribbon
scissors, tacky glue, X-acto® knife, Post-it® notes

Refer to page 41 to cover the card with the red with white dots Paper Pizazz™ and cut a 2½"x3½" piece from the center. Cut four ½"x4½" strips from the barnwood Cards In Minutes™ card. Lay them to frame the window and cut the corners at an angle so the strips don't overlap. Glue them in place. Cut three ⅛"x4" barnwood Cards In Minutes™ strips and glue inside the front flap for pane dividers. Stamp and emboss (see page 28) the snowman on the center back flap to show through the window. Open the card, mask the snowman (see page 29) and lightly sponge (see page 32) a blue hill. Sponge a blue sky. Stamp green trees on the hill. Use the Appliqué™ to make curves for hill mounds and snow on the trees. Sprinkle with glitter and let dry. Remove the mask and color the snowman. Stamp and emboss white snowflakes in the sky. Stamp pine boughs on sticker paper. Cut out and adhere to the card front window top. Tie the ribbon into a shoestring bow with 1" loops and 3½"-4" tails. Glue to the pine boughs as shown.

Border Stamps

Border stamp dies are molded with repeating images to create perfectly spaced designs anywhere on your project. Some are mounted on rollers (shown on page 8) and others are mounted on a long rectangle of wood. Often, the wood handled border stamps contain only one image that is intended to be repeatedly stamped in a line along the border of your project.

Creating a border on your project is easy—it's where you place the image that counts the most! Stamp a border to frame the focal point image (as shown at the top of page 18). Stamp borders on two sides of a project to accentuate the center image (such as the angel card at the top of page 109), or create a border along only one side of the project as shown at the bottom of page 113.

Border stamps are versatile, and don't only have to be used to make borders. The Medieval stampstick border image on the menu project on page 112 is not used as a border. Nor is the Heart border image on the invitation on the same page. The Fruit border image acts both as a focal point for the bookmark and a border for the card in the projects at the top of page 110. The same is true of the Strawberry stamp used to create a focal point for the box top and a border around the box in the hat box project on page 111.

Whether creating a border or using the image to adorn another area of your project, these stamps offer more images to add to your resources for expressing your creativity with rubber stamps.

This chapter's background paper is from Paper Pizazz™ Handmade Papers.

Congratulations, Baby!

stamps: Baby Border, "Fun Congratulations!"
pigment inks: black, turquoise
clear embossing powder, heat tool
cardstock: white, fuchsia
pastel dots patterned Paper Pizazz™
brush markers: pink, blue, purple, green
9" of ⅜" wide purple checked ribbon
ripple patterned scissors, straight edged scissors
foam mounting dots, tacky glue

Cut a 5⅛"x7¼" piece of fuchsia cardstock and make a top-folding card (see page 41). Use black ink to stamp and emboss (see page 28) a Baby Border around the edges of a 5"x3½" piece of pastel dots Paper Pizazz™. Color in the images. Stamp and emboss a turquoise "congratulations!" on the white cardstock. Use patterned scissors to trim around it and glue it to a piece of fuchsia cardstock. Trim it ⅛" larger. Use the ribbon to tie a shoestring bow with ¾" loops and 1½" tails and glue it above the word. Affix the word plaque to the center of the card with foam mounting dots.

Baby Goody Bag

stamps: Baby Border, Lower Case Alphabet Set
pigment inks: black, turquoise
cardstock: white, fuchsia
pastel dots patterned Paper Pizazz™
brush markers: pink, blue, purple, green
20" of ⅜" wide purple checked ribbon
cellophane bag and goodies to go inside
⅛" hole punch, tacky glue
ripple patterned scissors, straight edged scissors

Cut the white cardstock to the same width as the bag and to fold over approximately 3½" of the top (this one is 6"x7"). Cut the pastel dots Paper Pizazz™ to fit and glue it to the front of the cardstock. Use black ink to stamp and emboss (see page 28) a Baby Border along the bottom of the paper. Use the markers to color them in. Stamp and emboss the baby's name in turquoise on white cardstock, trim with patterned scissors and mat (see page 41) it on fuchsia cardstock. Trim the mat ⅛" larger and glue the plaque above the border. Fill the bag with the goodies, fold the card over the top and punch two holes through the card and bag just below the top and 4" apart. Thread the ribbon through the holes and tie it in a shoestring bow with 1½" loops and 3" tails.

Angel Card & Place Card

stamps: Sarah Angel, Country
Floral
black pigment ink
clear embossing powder
two 4¾"x5⅝" ivory cards
green checked patterned Paper
Pizazz™
sage green paper
ivory cardstock
watercolors: blue, red, green, light
blue, light green, maroon, brown,
peach, pink
black fine-tip permanent-ink pen
tacky glue, scissors
foam mounting dots, heat tool

For the card: Stamp and emboss (see page 28) Sarah Angel in black ink on cardstock. Color her in. Cut around her outline and use foam mounting dots to affix her to a 2¾"x4" green checked Paper Pizazz™ mat. Glue to one card front, then stamp and emboss a Country Floral border on each side. Color it in and use the pen to make dashes, slashes and dots along the card top and bottom. Glue the card back to solid paper and trim it ⅛" larger.

For the place card: Cut the remaining card to a 3⅞"x4" place card; save the remaining scraps. Cut green checked Paper Pizazz™ to fit and glue it to the front. Stamp and emboss the Country Floral image on a card scrap, write the guest's name below the stamp and cut it out as shown. Use the pen to echo the country themed dashed border as done on the card. Glue the name plate to the place card front.

Thank You Card

stamps: Accent Scroll Decorative, "Thank You"
red stamping paint
4½"x6" black card
cardstock: 2⅛"x2½" white, 2½"x2¾" red,
2¼"x2⅝" black
4¼"x5¾" piece of lace patterned Paper Pizazz™
tacky glue, scissors

This decorative stamp echoes the swirling letters of the word stamp and makes a perfect border for the card. Stamp the Accent Scroll image three times down the right lace Paper Pizazz™ side. Glue it to the card front. Stamp the "Thank You" image on white cardstock. Layer it on the black and red cardstock pieces, then glue it to the card front as shown.

Fruitful Bookmark & Card

stamps: Fruit Border, Maidenhair Fern, "Thinking of You"
pigment inks: green, black
clear embossing powder, heat tool
ivory cardstock: 5¼" square card, 2¼"x6"
*   strip, 1⅜"x4⅝" strip*
brown cardstock: 5½" square,
*   2½"x6¼" strip, 1⅝"x5" strip*
5⅛" square of dark green paper
watercolors: orange, green, peach,
*   red, lime*
6" long green tassel
deckle patterned scissors
straight edged scissors
#0 round paintbrush, X-acto® knife
¼" hole punch, pencil, ruler, tacky glue

For the bookmark: Round the corners of the 2¼"x6" cardstock strip. Stamp and emboss green Maidenhair Fern to cover it. Glue it on the large brown strip. Stamp and emboss the Fruit Border on the 1⅛"x4⅝" ivory strip, paint the image and trim with patterned scissors. Glue it on the remaining brown strip and trim these edges with patterned scissors. Glue the Fruit strip to the center. Punch a hole in the bookmark top. Thread the tassel through the hole inserting the tail through the loop to secure.

For the card: Cut a 1⁵⁄₁₆"x4⁷⁄₁₆" window ⅜" in from the green paper right edge. Cover the card (see page 41) with the green paper. Use the knife to cut a 1³⁄₁₆"x4⁵⁄₁₆" window in the card as shown. Stamp and emboss (see page 28) the Fruit Border stamp on the inside card to show through the window, and the word stamp left of the window. Paint the border image and a block of peach paint behind it to fill the window. Glue the card back to the brown square.

Flower Pot Card

stamps: Berry Border, "Fun to/from"
pigment inks: red, green
clear embossing powder, heat tool, brown brush marker
cardstock: 6"x10" light brown, 1⅝"x3¼" sage green
three 18" lengths of natural raffia, foam sponge
⅛" hole punch, scissors, tacky glue, tracing paper, pencil

Trace the pot pattern on page 142. Cut it out. Fold the light brown cardstock in half to make a 6"x5" top-folding card (see page 41). Place the pattern on the card fold and keep the top edges in tact as you cut a flower pot from brown cardstock. Apply ink to the appropriate portions of the stamp then stamp and emboss (see page 28) the Berry Border along the pot rim. Sponge (see page 32) the pot sides and bottom brown to add dimension to the card. Fold the sage green cardstock in half to make a card. Stamp and emboss the "to/from" image on a 1½" brown square and glue it to the sage green card front. Punch a hole in the corner. Handle the raffia as one and wrap it around the pot as shown. Tie it in a shoestring bow with 1½" loops and 2" tails, catching the tag in one strand.

Berry Border Hat Boxes

Decorative foam stamps: Strawberry Border, Leaf Border, Checkerboard, Strawberry

stamping paints: white, sage, green, red, yellow, pale blue, black

papier mâché hat boxes: 11¾"x5⅝", 9¼"x5", 7"x3⅛"

1 yard of yellow & white striped self-adhesive wallpaper

1⅞ yards of ⅝" wide black & white checked ribbon

paintbrushes: 1" wide, ¼" wide

scissors, wallpaper glue

new pencil with eraser, foam sponges

For the large box: Cut a 5"x37½" strip of wallpaper to fit around the box. Lay it out flat, patterned side up. Apply red, green and pale blue paints to the appropriate portions of the Strawberry Border stamp and impress the image along the length of the wallpaper strip. Let it dry and glue the strip around the box. Paint the lid top yellow and the lid sides white. Let dry. Apply black paint to the Checkerboard image and stamp it around the lid sides. Let dry.

top view

For the medium box: Paint the box yellow, the lid top sage and the lid sides white; let dry. Apply green paint to the Leaf Border image and stamp it around the box sides. Use the ¼" paintbrush to paint black stripes ⅛" apart around the lid sides.

For the small box: Paint the box and lid top white; paint the lid sides black. Apply red and green paint to the appropriate portions of the Strawberry image and stamp it around the box sides. Stamp two images on the lid top as shown at left. Dip the pencil eraser into white paint and touch to the lid sides to make dots. Let dry. Stack the three boxes and use the ribbon to bind them together tying a shoestring bow (see page 41) with 2½" loops and 5" tails.

Menu & Heart Embossed Card

stamps: Heart Border, "Menu", Medieval Stampstick
ivory cardstock: 5¼"x7½" piece, two 4"x1⅞" pieces
Paper Pizazz™: vellum, antique laces
clear embossing ink, gold embossing powder, heat tool
gold acrylic paint, foam sponge, old toothbrush
5"x7" gold frame with a 4½"x6½" opening
access to a computer and printer
24" of ⅝" wide gold wire mesh ribbon
bone folder, spray bottle with water, tacky glue
scallop patterned scissors, straight edged scissors

For the menu: Type the menu into the computer and print it onto the vellum Paper Pizazz™. Stamp and emboss (see page 28) the "Menu" and Medieval images as shown. Cut the vellum and antique lace Paper Pizazz™ to fit and put them in the frame.

For the card: Fold the large ivory piece into a top-folding card (see page 41). To spatter the card front, dip the moistened toothbrush in gold paint and pull your thumb across the bristles. Sponge gold paint onto a small ivory piece and let dry. Spray one side of the remaining cardstock piece with water, lay the wet side onto the die side of the Heart stamp and use the bone folder to burnish the image into the cardstock and let dry. Trim it with patterned scissors and mat it on the gold cardstock. Glue to the front of the card. Tie the ribbon around the front card flap top in a shoestring bow with 1" loops and 4" tails. Wrap the tails to the inside of the card and glue to secure. Trim ¼" from the lower front card with patterned scissors and sponge gold paint along the visible inside back flap. Let dry.

Embossed Frame & Invitation

stamps: Border #1, Icon, "Invitation"
clear embossing ink, gold embossing powder, heat tool
mat board pieces: 7¼"x6½" tan, 7¼"x6½" black,
  3"x6" black strip
ivory parchment: 6"x4½" card, 3½"x1½" strip
Paper Pizazz™ crushed suede patterned papers: blue, green,
  burgundy, copper
specialty gold metallic Paper Pizazz™, vellum Paper Pizazz™
24" of ⅛" wide gold cording
4 gold pony beads, 2 gold flute beads
X-acto® knife, tacky glue, tracing paper, pencil
heartbeat patterned scissors, straight edged scissors

For the frame: Remove a 3¾"x 3⅛" piece from the tan mat board center. Stamp and emboss (see page 28) four Border images and four Icon images each on different crushed suede Paper Pizazz™ papers. Cut the border images to 1½"x3⅛" and the Icons to 1½" squares. Glue evenly spaced around the frame opening. Glue three sides to the black mat board leaving the top open to slip a photo in. Trace the pattern on page 141 to cut a frame support from the remaining mat board and glue to the frame back.

For the invitation: Cut the vellum Paper Pizazz™ to fit and fold over the card. Stamp and emboss the lower vellum edge with the Border #1 image. Trim below the image. Stamp and emboss the "Invitation" image on the ivory strip, trim with patterned scissors and mat on gold paper. Trim it ⅛" larger and glue to the card front center. Tie the cording around the card fold and knot on the right side as shown. Thread beads on each end as shown and knot the ends to secure. Line the inside card bottom with a 6"x1" gold paper strip.

Paper Ribbon & Birthday Card

stamps: Medieval Border, "Happy Birthday"
black pigment ink
gift box, black wrapping paper
⅝" wide red checked ribbon
cardstock: black, red, ivory
kraft paper, ruler
scissors, tacky glue
foam mounting tape
black fine-tip permanent-ink pen

For the ribbon: Wrap the gift in black wrapping paper. Repeatedly stamp the Border image along a 1½" wide strip of kraft paper. Cut the ivory stock 1⅝" wide and the red 1⅞" wide. Cut the red, ivory and kraft papers long enough to wrap once around your gift box. Layer the papers and glue to secure. Wrap the red checked ribbon around the gift box and tie a shoe-string bow (see page 41). Wrap the paper ribbon around the gift and glue the ends to secure.

For the card: Stamp a square Medieval Border frame on a 5¾"x5¼" piece of kraft paper. Stamp the "Happy

Birthday" image on a 2¾"x2¼" piece of ivory and glue it on a 3"x2½" piece of black. Use the pen and ruler to draw a square border ⅛" in from the edge. Use foam mounting tape to affix it to the center. Mat it on red trimming ⅛" larger. Fold a 6"x11¼" piece of black cardstock into a top-folding card (see page 41). Glue the frame to the card front.

Heart Border Card

Ribbon Heart Border stamp
brush markers: red, black
6⅛"x4½" ivory card
6⁵⁄₁₆"x4⅝" piece of red cardstock
6⅛"x1½" strip of black handmade paper
½ yard of ⅝" wide black & tan checked fabric
tacky glue, scissors

Color the hearts red and the swirls black on the Border stamp and impress the image across the lower front card flap. Cut away the card flap below the stamp. Tear one long edge of the black strip and glue it to the inside lower back flap. Glue the card to the red cardstock. Glue a 6⅛" long ribbon strip along the card top. Use the remaining ribbon to tie a shoestring bow (see page 41) with 1½" loops and 2½" tails. Glue the bow to the ribbon center.

Roller & Mini Stamps

This chapter features two kinds of stamps—roller stamps and mini stamps. Roller stamps come in lots of great images and are perfect for creating borders or other accents to your projects (such as the cat tracks at the top of page 118). Mini stamps have just as much detail and come in many images—they're just smaller! They're perfect for decorating tiny projects like the cards on page 127. As you'll see in this chapter, mini stamps don't mean mini projects—nor do roller stamps have to roll only borders!

A roller stamp was used to create the very unique, woven card on page 116. A roller stamp also created the meandering puppy steps across the background paper of the scrapbook page at the bottom of page118. These are just two examples of roller stamps being used to create wonderful patterns that are anything but borders!

A terrific example of using mini stamps on a large project comes on page 122. This country-style doll chair looks perfect with the many small rose buds that embellish it.

Mini stamps, while small, can be used to achieve the same effects we've mentioned throughout this book! Create a springtime background as shown in the projects on page 120. Or establish a strong focal point like the bagalopes on page 122 or the kitty bookmark on page 125. Mini stamps can be used to create a wonderful scene as shown in the "thanks!" card on page 127. And they can delicately accent a word stamp illustrated on the anniversary card on page 128.

Regardless of how you use roller or mini stamp images, they can provide the same warm, whimsical, serious or romantic feelings the other stamps in this book do. They offer you more choices for using just the right image to express your thoughts, feelings and creativity.

This chapter's background paper is from Paper Pizazz™ Handmade Papers.

Puffy Hearts Lampshade

stamps: Hearts roller, Heart in a Heart
pink dye-based ink
6" tall lampshade kit
acrylic paints: pink, lavender
white Liquid Appliqué™
#2 round paintbrush
heat tool
scissors, stapler

Lay the lampshade paper flat. Stamp roller Hearts along the top and bottom shade edges. Stamp three Heart in a Heart images evenly spaced between the Heart borders. Cover each heart image with applique and let it dry overnight. Apply heat to the Appliqué™ hearts until they puff up. Dilute the paint colors, mixing one part paint with one part water, and paint each as shown. Let dry. Wrap the shade around the support and staple the seam to secure.

Embossed Heart Frame

stamps: Hearts roller, Heart
white pigment ink, white embossing powder, heat tool
Paper Pizazz™ patterned papers: pink & blue plaid,
*   stitching on pink, tri-dots on pink, pink hearts on blue,*
*   lavender plaid*
solid color papers: pink, lavender
mat board pieces: 5¾"x4¾" pink, 2½"x3½" white
X-acto® knife, ruler, scissors, tacky glue, photograph

Stamp and emboss (see page 28) four Hearts onto the pink & blue plaid Paper Pizazz™. Cut them to 1⅛" squares. Stamp and emboss a strip of rolled Hearts on each remaining sheet of patterned Paper Pizazz™. Cut two 3"x¾"six-heart strips and two 2"x¾" four-heart strips. Glue the strips and squares onto the lavender paper in a rectangle as shown. Cut out the frame leaving a ⅛" wide lavender edge around the outside. Cut the pink paper to 5¾"x4¾" and glue the lavender rectangle in the center. Use the knife to remove the center leaving a ⅛" wide lavender edge around the inside. Glue three sides to the pink mat board leaving the top open to slip in a photo. Glue upper ½" of the small mat board piece to the frame back for the support piece.

Paper Quilt Card

Quilt Pattern roller stamp
pigment inks: purple, pink
clear embossing powder, heat tool
pink tiles patterned Paper Pizazz™
solid color papers: white, purple
10½"x5¼" white cardstock
X-acto® knife, ruler, tacky glue, scissors

Refer to page 41 to fold the cardstock into a card. Cut the sheet of pink tiles Paper Pizazz™ to fit, and glue to the card front. Stamp and emboss three 5½" long purple and two 5½" long pink Quilt Pattern strips onto white paper. Cut each strip to 5". Measuring from the card spine on the left, cut a 4⅞" long slit into the card front at these placements: 1¹⁄₁₆", 1½", 2⅜", 2⅞" 3¾" and 4¼". Weave a purple strip under the slits and glue in place. Weave a pink strip over the slits and glue in place. Repeat to weave the remaining strips as shown. Glue the card to purple paper and cut it to a 5½" square.

Gift Bag & Topper

*stamps: Quilt Pattern roller, Accent Heart
  Decorative, Uppercase Alphabet Set
white pigment ink, white embossing powder
5¼"x8"gift bag, 5¼"x7¼" fuchsia cardstock
stamping paints: white, fuchsia
new pencil with eraser, foam sponges, scissors
tacky glue, cardboard, heat tool*

For the topper: Fold the cardstock in half length-wise then stamp and emboss the Quilt Pattern image to border the front masking (see page 29) where necessary. Stamp and emboss letters to spell the recipient's name in the center. Cut a slit along the fold keeping ¼" intact at each side.

For the bag: Keep the bag folded and insert a piece of cardboard. Randomly stamp fuchsia Accent Hearts on the bag front. Let dry. To make the dots, dip the pencil eraser into white paint then randomly touch it in each heart. Let dry. To put the topper on the bag, slip the bag handles through the slit in the topper.

Heart Memory Page

*stamps: Hearts roller, Bold Heart
fuchsia pigment ink, clear embossing powder, heat tool
pink moiré patterned Paper Pizazz™
acid-free solid color papers: lavender, pastel purple
white photo corners, archival quality glue
ripple patterned scissors, straight edged scissors
sheet protector, 3-ring binder album
3 photographs, pencil, X-acto® knife*

Cut the photos with patterned scissors to focus on the subjects. Mat (see page 41) them onto pastel purple paper. Arrange on the moiré patterned Paper Pizazz™ and lightly mark their placement with a pencil. Stamp and emboss (see page 28) roller Hearts ¼" inside the edges of the patterned paper. Stamp and emboss four Bold Heart images. Stamp three of them to overlap where the photos will be. Use the knife to cut around the parts of the Hearts that overlap the photo areas. Slip the matted photos under the Hearts and affix the photo corners as shown. Cut around the Heart border. Glue the page to the lavender paper. Slip into the sheet protector then into the album.

Kitty Card

Kitty Card

stamps: Cat Tracks roller, Thomas,
  Frisky Kitten, Cat Face, Paw
black pigment ink
clear embossing powder, heat tool
5¼" square white card
tan argyle patterned Paper Pizazz™
5½" square of black cardstock
brush markers: brown, gray, orange,
  yellow, purple, pink, green, lime
scissors, tacky glue, ruler, pencil

Cut four ½" wide tan argyle Paper Pizazz™ strips into the following lengths: 5¼", two 3⅛" and 1¾". Glue to the card front as shown. Stamp and emboss (see page 28) each kitty image, the Paw print and the Cat Tracks as shown. Color in the kitty images. Use the brush markers to make dots in groups of three, four and five, and to make dotted spirals in the empty areas as shown. Glue the card to the black cardstock.

Paw Frame

stamps: Cat Tracks roller, Paw
black pigment ink, clear embossing powder, heat tool
solid color papers: red, blue, yellow, teal, purple
5½" square piece of red mat board
white cardstock pieces: 5¼" square, 2½"x3¼"
tacky glue, tracing paper, pencil, ruler, photograph

Cut out a 3⅛" square from the center of the large white cardstock. Cut a ¾"x5" strip of each colored paper. Stamp and emboss the Cat Tracks image onto each. Glue the strips around the white square as shown. Stamp and emboss four Paw prints onto blue. Cut each to a 1⅛" square and glue to each corner. Glue three sides of the frame to the red mat board leaving the top open to slip in a photo. Trace the pattern on page 141 and cut a support from the small white cardstock. Glue to the frame back.

Paw Print Scrapbook Page

stamps: Cat Tracks roller, Paw
pigment inks: black, red, yellow, green, purple
acid-free solid color papers: green, purple, yellow, white,
  2 pieces of red
acid-free white cardstock
sheet protector, 3-ring binder album
scissors, archival quality glue, 3 photos

Cut the photos to focus on the subjects in them. Mat (see page 41) them on colored paper as shown. Stamp and emboss (see page 28) seven black Paw images on cardstock. Cut each out leaving a 2½" square area below one to write on. Write names and the date as shown. Cover the white paper with rolled Cat Tracks of different colors. Remember to clean the stamp between each color, and let each track dry before crossing it with another colored track. Cut the paper to 8¼"x 10¾" and glue to the remaining red sheet. Mat the journalled paw piece on yellow. Arrange the pieces on the background sheet and glue in place. Glue an embossed Paw print to each photo corner as shown. Slip into the sheet protector then into the album.

Love Card

stamps: Quilt Pattern roller, Elegant "Love"
red pigment ink, clear embossing powder, heat tool
5¼" square white card, white cardstock
red stripes patterned Paper Pizazz™
scissors, heart template
pencil with eraser, tacky glue

Cut the red stripes Paper Pizazz™ to fit and glue to the card front. Use the template to cut a heart from the card front center. Lightly draw the Heart shape onto the inside back card flap and open the card. Stamp and emboss (see page 28) the "Love" image inside the penciled heart. Erase the lines. Stamp and emboss four 5" long strips of the Quilt Pattern image onto cardstock. Trim each to 5"x⅞" and glue to frame the heart window on the card front.

Anniversary Card

stamps: Hearts roller, Elegant "Happy Anniversary"
pigment inks: red, black
clear embossing powder, heat tool
cardstock: 6"x9" white, 6"x 4¾" black, 6"x 1½" red
6"x3¼" piece of white with red dots patterned
  Paper Pizazz™
9" of ⅞" wide black & white checked ribbon
pencil, eraser, tacky glue, X-acto® knife

Fold the white cardstock to make a top-folding card (see page 41). Glue the white with red dots Paper Pizazz™ to the card front top. Use the knife to cut a 5⅜"x¾" window in the lower front card flap. Glue the red strip behind the window and cut a 5¼"x⅝" window into it. Lightly draw the window shape onto the inside back card flap and open the card. Stamp and emboss (see page 28) a red Hearts roller image in the penciled window area. Erase the lines. Glue the card to the black cardstock. Stamp and emboss a black "Happy Anniversary" in the white with red dots Paper Pizazz™ center. Tie the ribbon into a shoestring bow with 1½" loops and 2" tails. Glue as shown.

Ladybug Thank You

stamps: Ladybug, Bee, "Thank You"
black pigment ink, clear embossing powder, heat tool
5¼" white card with envelope
3"x2½" piece of white cardstock, red paper
black & white checked patterned Paper Pizazz™
brush markers: goldenrod, red, yellow, gray, black
scissors, tacky glue, ruler

For the envelope: Use the black marker to draw black dashed lines along the envelope flap. Color the Bee stamp black then impress the image onto the flap as shown. Color his body yellow and wings gray.

For the card: Turn the card with the fold at the top. Cut a free-form wavy line ½" above the bottom front card flap. Color a goldenrod border above it, then draw a black line as shown. Cut a ¾" tall red paper strip and glue it along the bottom back card flap. Cut a ⅛" wide single row of black & white checked Paper Pizazz™ and glue it on the red strip. Trim both to fit the card width. Randomly stamp and emboss (See page 28) black Ladybugs to cover the card. Color the Ladybugs red or goldenrod. Trim a wavy border around the cardstock piece. Stamp and emboss the "Thank You" image then draw a goldenrod border around it. Mat (see page 41) it on red. Glue it to the card center.

Happy Spring Card

stamps: Tulip, "Happy Spring"
black pigment ink, clear embossing powder
4½"x6" white card
3¾"x2" piece of white cardstock
black & white checked patterned Paper Pizazz™
4"x2¼" piece of black paper
brush markers: pink, green, goldenrod, yellow, red
tacky glue, scissors, heat tool, ruler

Turn the card with the fold at the top. Cut a free-form wavy line ½" above the bottom front card flap. Color a pink border above it, then draw a black line as shown. Color a 1" tall goldenrod strip along the bottom back card flap. Cut a ⅛" wide single row of black & white checked Paper Pizazz™ and glue it on the colored strip. Trim it to fit the card width. Randomly stamp and emboss (see page 28) the Tulip image to cover the card. Color as shown. Stamp and emboss "Happy Spring" on the cardstock. Trim a wavy border around it. Mat (see page 41) it on black. Color the images as shown and glue it to the card center.

Flower & Bug Notes

stamps: Spring Flower,
    Bee, Daisy, Sunflower,
    Ladybug, Butterfly,
    Dragonfly
dye-based inks: black,
    orange
white cardstock
brush markers: salmon, red,
    yellow, lime, pink, blue,
    green, orange, purple
9" of ⅜" wide red checked ribbon
black fine-tip pen, X-acto® knife
straight edged scissors, ruler
patterned scissors: pinking, jumbo scallop

These cute little note cards are simple to make and lots of fun to color in. With these tiny images full of bright color, there's no need to mask the images as is shown with the Bee and Daisy card. Orange Daisies were stamped first and the black Bee and Dragonfly images easily cover them. To make interesting borders like the green one on the Bee note, trim a piece of cardstock with patterned scissors (pinking scissors were used here). Use the trimmed cardstock for a border template (see page 32), but color it with brush markers instead of foam sponges.

For the note cards: Cut a piece of cardstock to 3¼"x7". Cut as many note cards as you'd like! Fold the note card down 2" below the top and use scalloped scissors to taper one short edge—this is the top flap. Fold the note card up 2⅜" above the bottom for the bottom flap. Make a 1" long slit widthwise ¾" above the bottom edge to tuck the top flap into when closed. To stamp the card, unfold it and turn it so the back side is up and the top flap is nearest you (this way, your stamped images will be right side up when you fold it closed!). Stamp the images using black ink and color them in with brush markers. Stamp them randomly, like the Daisies and Butterflies, or in a row like the Spring Flowers and Ladybugs. Use the black pen to draw dashed lines around the card front, wavy lines around the top flap, or motion dots behind a flying bug. Bundle the cards together and tie them with the ribbon.

Heart & Bee Stationery

stamps: Heart, Bee
black waterproof ink
6"x9" pieces of white paper
watercolors: red, yellow, gray
black fine-tip pen, ruler

Create a fun spring border along the top of stationery paper for letters with a personal touch! Stamp the Heart and Bee images along the paper top as shown. Paint in with watercolors. Use the pen to draw a dashed border around each image.

Doll Chair

stamps: Flowers Desk Set
black crafter's ink
6¾"x15"x6¾" unfinished wood doll chair
acrylic paints: pink, green, yellow, black, sage green, ivory
paintbrushes: 1" wide flat, ⅛" wide flat, #2" round
Post-it® notes, foam sponges, acrylic wood sealer, masking tape

Prepare the wood (see page 36). Paint a 1½" ivory square in the top slat center. Let dry. Paint a 1" yellow square in its center. Let it dry and stamp a flower image. Paint the flower as shown. Paint the remaining top slat and the leg cross bars black. Paint the middle slat ivory let dry and stamp random blossoms on it. Paint the bottom slat yellow, let dry and stamp three rose images on it. Paint the images as shown. Paint a 4⅞" square on the seat center yellow. Let dry. Paint a ⅛" ivory border around it. Let dry. Mask (see page 29) it, then paint the remaining chair sage green. Let it dry and remove the mask. Apply tape to protect the seat edges and randomly stamp the rose blossom image in the yellow square. Paint them pink and green. Remove the tape. Paint ⅛" wide checks around each leg base and upper back legs as shown. Dip a paintbrush handle in yellow paint and touch it to the top slat for dots. Paint ⅛" wide black squares around the ivory border on the top slat and seat center for checks. Paint the seat edge ivory. Let dry. Paint ¾" wide strips for checks as shown. Let dry. Seal the chair.

Leaf Bagalopes

Leaf Tray stamps
dye-based inks: black, green
four 5"x7" white envelopes (gloss-coated or matte)
two 2½"x2¾" pieces of dark green handmade paper
two 2"x2½" pieces of light green paper
two 1¾"x2" pieces of white gloss-coated paper
brush markers: green, light green
patterned scissors: zipper, scallop, pinking, ripple
ruler, stylus, straight edged scissors
tacky glue, double-stick tape

Transform an envelope into a gift bag in minutes! Seal the envelope. Randomly stamp leaf images to cover the front of two envelopes. Use brush markers to color in the leaves, or leave them uncolored as shown. Use the stylus to score the envelope, front and back, ½" in from each of three sides. Cut ½" from the fourth. Cut a short end for a tall narrow bagalope. Cut a long end for a wide short bagalope. Cut the top edge with patterned scissors for interest. Crease along the scored lines, open the bagalope then push the envelope edges in. Fold the corners under and secure with double-stick tape. Stamp a single leaf image on each white paper piece and trim with patterned scissors. Double mat (see page 41) each onto colored paper. Glue to the bag fronts as shown.

Veggie Dip & Recipe Cards

Vegetable Tray Stamp Set
black waterproof ink
natural recipe cards, 6"x7" natural card
watercolors: purple, green, red, brown, tan
18" of ⅝" wide green satin ribbon
5½" wide cellophane bag
dry vegetable soup mix
paintbrushes: #2 round, #0 liner
black fine-tip pen, tape, ¼" hole punch

Stamp vegetable images along the top of the 6"x7" card and in each recipe card corner. Paint them with watercolors and paint a ¾" block of color behind each. Use the pen to write the recipe, drawing a dot at each letter end as shown.

For the recipe write: Veggie Dip, 2 cups Sour Cream, 1 cup Mayo, 1 packet dry Veggie soup mix. Blend together and chill 2 hours—Serve with raw vegies.

For the soup write: Mix well with 3 cups boiling water. Let stand 5 mins.

To make the veggie pack: Fill the bag with vegetable soup mix. Fold the top down and tape to secure. Slip the top of the bag into the card and punch two holes through the card and bag as shown. Thread the ribbon from back to front and tie a shoe-string bow (see page 41) with 2" loops and 3" tails.

Les Petits Pois Gift Bag

Vegetable Tray Stamp Set
black waterproof ink
5" square kraft gift bag with handles, purple tissue paper
watercolors: green, lime, purple
paintbrushes: ¼" wide flat, #2 round
black fine-tip pen
pencil, ruler, cardboard

Keep the bag folded and insert a piece of cardboard. Use the ruler and pencil to lightly draw a 3" square in the bag center and a 4⅜" square around it. Divide the inner square into sixteen ¾" squares. Stamp a pea image in every other square and paint the rest purple. Let dry. Paint the pea images green. Paint the outer square lime. Let dry. Use the pen to draw a —•— border as shown. Write "les petits pois" ("the little peas") in the lime border. Remove the cardboard and insert the tissue paper.

Puppy Treat Box & Tag

Dogs Desk Set stamps
black pigment ink, clear embossing powder, heat tool
3"x4"x3" white gift box with an oval window and handle
solid color papers: 4"x6" black, 1½" square of white
cardstock: 1½" square of black, 1⅜" square of tan,
3¼"x1⅝" red
brush markers: red, brown, black
5" of ⅛" wide black checked ribbon
⅛" hole punch, ripple patterned scissors
Post-it® notes, tacky glue
black fine-tip permanent-ink pen

For the box: Lay the flattened gift box on a hard surface and mask (see page 29) the window. Stamp and emboss (see page 28) the "WOOF!" Paw image to cover the box. Cut the black paper to fit and cover the box top flaps. Color the handles with the red marker. Use the red marker to make dots around the window. Remove the mask and fold the box.

For the card: Stamp the dog image on the white paper. Color as shown. Trim with patterned scissors, draw black dots around the edges and glue to the tan cardstock. Glue this to the black cardstock. Fold the red cardstock in half widthwise and glue the matted dog image to the front. Punch a hole in the upper left corner and thread the ribbon through it. Fill the box with doggie treats, close the lid and tie the ribbon to the handle as shown.

Puppy Frame

Dogs Desk Set Stamps
black pigment ink, clear embossing powder
four 1" squares of red cardstock
4¾" square of tan cardstock
5" square of black mat board
2"x3¾" strip of black mat board
brush markers: brown, red, light brown
heat tool, X-acto® knife
tacky glue, photograph

Stamp and emboss (see page 28) a "WOOF!" Paw image on each red square. Glue one to each corner of the tan square. Cut a 2⅜" square opening in the center. Alternately stamp and emboss the puppy head and doggie images around the tan square as shown. Color in the images. Glue three sides of the tan square to the black mat board leaving the top open to slip in a photo. Slip in your photo. Glue the upper ½" of the mat board strip to the frame back for a support.

Kitty Album

Cats Desk Stamp Set
black pigment ink, clear embossing powder
8"x5¼" pieces of mat board: 1 red, 1 black
lavender paper
purple watercolor, #2 round paintbrush
18" of ⅛" wide black velvet ribbon
two red grommets & grommet tool
X-acto® knife, tacky glue, filler paper
2" photograph, heat tool, ruler, scissors

Cut the filler paper to 6½"x5". Cut
the lavender paper to a 2¼"x5¼"
strip and a 3"x2⅝" rectangle.
Remove a 1¾"x1½" piece from the
rectangle center. Paint ¾" squares of purple in
a checkerboard pattern on the strip. Paint ½" purple
squares around the frame as shown. Stamp and emboss
(see page 28) a paw print in the center of each watercolored
square. Glue the strip along the left side of the red mat board. Stamp and
emboss cats on the remaining red mat board. Glue the frame over the photo
onto the mat board as shown. Insert the filler paper between the two mat boards.
Follow the manufacturer's instructions to use the tool and insert the grommets 3" apart in
the center of the lavender strip. Thread the ribbon through the holes from back to front and
tie it into a shoestring bow (see page 41) with 2" loops and tails.

Kitty Bookmark

stamps: Duffy Kitty, Cats Desk set, Cat Tracks roller
black waterproof ink, #2 paintbrush
2⅝"x6⅜" black cardstock
2⅜"x6⅛" brown cardstock
2¼"x6" ivory cardstock
black & white checked patterned Paper Pizazz™
watercolors: blue, brown, red, tan, orange, green
6" long black tassel
tacky glue, scissors, ¼" wide hole punch

Cut ⅛" wide strips of black & white checked Paper
Pizazz™ to the following lengths: five 2¼", two 6",
one 1¼", two 1". Lay them to divide the bookmark
as shown, then use the pencil to lightly draw each
section. Stamp the images in each section as shown
and paint them. Let dry. Paint the backgrounds and
let dry. Lightly paint tan onto the patterned paper
strips. Let dry. Glue them to divide the bookmark
sections as shown and round the corners. Glue the
bookmark to the brown cardstock and then to the
black. Punch a hole ½" from the top, thread the
tassel through and thread the end through the loop
to secure.

Java Journal

Java Desk Stamp Set
pigment inks: black, brown, mustard
clear embossing powder, heat tool
4¼"x6¼" journal
kraft paper, ivory paper
brush markers: brown, tan
X-acto® knife, ruler, scissors, tacky glue

Center the journal on the kraft paper and cut a 10"x7½" piece. Fold and glue ½" of the short right side around the back cover edge, wrap it around the journal and fold the remaining ½" into the front cover edge. Glue to secure (see page 41 for covering a card tips). Miter the corners (see page 56). Stamp and emboss (see page 28) the "Java bean" stamp across the journal top. Repeat ¾" below the top row. Continue to stamp rows ¾" apart to the journal bottom. Alternately stamp and emboss cup and pot images on four 4¼" wide strips of ivory paper. Cut each to ¾" tall. Glue them to the journal cover as shown. Color the beans and coffee cup as shown.

Mini Cards

Let's Do Lunch Stamp Set
pigment inks: black, brown
clear embossing powder, heat tool
cardstock, two 2¾" square slate blue, two 2¾" rose,
   four 6"x3" brown
ivory paper, tracing paper, watercolor paper
watercolors: yellow, pink, blue, red, tan
pencil, #2 paintbrush, 9" of jute twine, ruler, scissors

Tear four 2½" squares of watercolor paper. Use the ruler and pencil to lightly divide each into nine ¾" squares. Paint 5 squares with a watercolor and stamp a "Coffee Time" or "Happy Hour" image in the remaining squares as shown. Paint each image. Glue the "Coffee Time" squares to slate blue cardstock and the "Happy Hour" squares to rose cardstock. Fold each brown piece in half to make a card (see page 41) and glue a matted piece to each. Trace the envelope pattern on page 142. Cut and fold them from ivory paper. Glue to secure. Bind the cards and envelopes with twine and knot to secure.

Dragonfly Notebook

stamps: Dragonfly, Tulip, Flower, Leaf, Sun, Bee,
  Ladybug, Star
brown waterproof ink
4"x5" piece of watercolor paper
4⅜"x5" spiral bound notebook
watercolors: red, brown, orange, yellow, blue, black, tan
paintbrushes: #2 liner, #2 round
tacky glue, scissors

Stamp the Dragonfly image in the center of the
watercolor paper. Stamp the remaining images to surround it as shown. Paint each image. Paint blocks of
color around each image leaving a 1¾"x2½" opening
around the dragonfly. Paint tiny shapes between
them as shown and let dry. Glue the
watercolor paper to the notebook front.

Thanks! Card

stamps: Flowers Desk Set, Bugs Desk Set, Heart, Bee, Leaf,
  Stick Dot Alphabet Set
black waterproof ink
6⅜"x4½" white card, watercolor paper, lavender paper
peach plaid patterned Paper Pizazz™
brush markers: red, lavender, orange
watercolors: red, purple, pink, orange, yellow, lime, green,
  blue, teal
#2 round paintbrush, Post-it® notes, ruler, pencil
deckle patterned scissors, straight edged scissors, tacky glue

Cover the card front with lavender paper (see page
41). Cut the watercolor paper ¼" smaller than the
card front. Divide into five unequal sections. Mask
(see page 29) each remaining section as you work in
another. Stamp a variety of images in each section
as shown. Paint the images then paint color behind
them in strips, squares, plaids and solids. Stamp
two bee images on a 1¾"x2" piece of paper, mat on
lavender and trim with patterned scissors. Stamp a
heart on a 1" square of peach plaid Paper Pizazz™.
Glue to the card front. Let dry and use brush markers
to color the letters and stamp "thanks!"

Teeny Tags & Envelopes

Stamp Sets: My Heart Is For You, Write Soon, Bon Voyage
black waterproof ink, blue crafter's ink
solid color papers: rose, pink, purple, lavender, sage green,
  white, blue
watercolor paper, tracing paper, pencil, tacky glue
watercolors: yellow, brown, green, red, purple, orange, blue,
  pink, peach
paintbrushes: #2 liner, #0 round
mini scallop patterned scissors, straight edged scissors

For the envelopes: Trace the pattern on page 142
and cut them from rose and pink papers. Fold them
and glue to secure. Stamp a black "Write Soon" and
blue "Express Delivery" image on the outside of one
or a "visit soon" image on the inside as shown. To
make an envelope liner, cut a 2⅞"x4⅝" piece of
watercolor paper. Round the upper 1½" to follow the
curve of the envelope flap. Stamp images and paint
as shown.

For the cards: Stamp a single image, four images in
a block or three in a line on watercolor paper as
shown. Color them and tear or cut around them.
Glue to solid color paper. Or paint a square of paper
with blocks of color and glue to it. Mat (see page 41)
and trim with patterned scissors for variety.

Quilt Card & Gift Box

stamps: Heart, Bee, Tulip, Flower
clear embossing ink
gold embossing powder, heat tool
5¼" square white card
5" long tube gift box, white paper
Paper Pizazz™ patterned papers: pink hearts
    on blue, yellow diamonds, tri-dots on pink,
    mint swirl
acrylic paints: green, pink, purple, yellow
sheer purple ribbon: 20" of ¼" wide,
    9" of ⅝" wide
⅝" wide purple button, yellow thread
metallic gold pen
tacky glue, paintbrushes: #2 flat, #0 liner
deckle patterned scissors, straight edged scissors

For the card: Cover the card (see page 41) front with yellow diamonds Paper Pizazz™. Dilute 1 part green paint with 1 part water and paint diagonal stripes on the white paper. Let dry. Use patterned scissors to cut a 5" square and draw gold dots around the edges with the pen. Glue it to the card front. Cut a 4¼" pink hearts on blue square with patterned scissors, draw gold around the edges. Stamp and emboss (see page 28) an image on each piece of Paper Pizazz™ and paint as shown. Cut each with patterned scissors to a 1⅜" square. Draw around the edges with the gold pen. Glue each contrasting paper and cut to 1". Glue to the card front as shown. Use the gold pen to make dotted borders as shown.

Tie the wide ribbon into a shoestring bow with 2" loops and 3" tails and glue as shown. Tie thread in the button and glue to the bow center.

For the box: Cut patterned Paper Pizazz™ to fit and cover the box sides and ends. Follow the instructions for the card to paint green diagonal stripes on white paper. Stamp and emboss a Heart on painted green paper. Paint it as shown. Cut it with patterned scissors to a 1⅜" square. Glue it to a 1⅝" square of yellow diamond paper and glue it to the box front. Tie the ribbon around the box in a shoestring bow with 1" loops and 2" tails. Use the pen to make gold dots around the box edges.

"Happy Anniversary" Card

stamps: Elegant "Happy Anniversary",
    Medieval Stampstick
clear embossing ink, gold embossing powder, heat tool
tapestry patterned Paper Pizazz™
5⅝"x8¾" white cardstock, 4½"x5¾" red cardstock
12" of 2mm metallic gold cording
metallic gold paint, foam sponge, clear tape
heartbeat patterned scissors, straight edged scissors

Refer to page 41 and use the white cardstock to make a top-folding card. Cut the tapestry Paper Pizazz™ to fit and glue to the front. Trim away ¼" from the bottom front flap with patterned scissors. Sponge (see page 32) a ½" wide gold border on the inside back flap. Stamp and emboss (see page 28) "Happy Anniversary" on the front card center. Stamp and emboss a border of seven Medieval images evenly spaced along the card front flap bottom. Wrap the cording around the front card flap as shown and secure it with tape inside. Glue the card to the red cardstock piece.

"Happy Holidays" Card

stamps: Funky Ornament, Funky "Happy Holidays"
black waterproof ink
white cardstock pieces: 2½"x1½", 1½"x4"
Christmas plaid patterned Cards In Minutes™ pieces:
    2¾"x1⅞", 2"x4⅛"
6½"x4½" Pine Boughs patterned Cards In Minutes™
red & white fabric pieces: 3⅛"x2⅜", 2½"x4⅜", 12"x1¼"
tacky glue, brush markers: green, red, yellow
straight edged scissors, patterned scissors: deckle, pinking

Trim each Christmas plaid and cardstock piece with
deckle scissors. Tear the long edges of the fabric strip
and tie it in a shoestring bow (see page 41) with 1¼" loops and 2"
tails. Trim the tails diagonally. Trim the remaining fabric pieces with pinking scissors.
Stamp the images onto the white pieces and color them as shown. Glue them to the card front as shown.

Blue & Gold Card

Italian stampstick
clear embossing ink, gold embossing powder, heat tool
blue tiles patterned Paper Pizazz™
5¼" square white card; 5½" square of red cardstock
tacky glue, scissors

Cut the blue tiles Paper Pizazz™ to fit and glue onto the
card front. Stamp and emboss (see page 28) the image
onto the card front in the pattern shown. Glue the card
to the red cardstock.

Bookmark & Box

stampsticks: Primitive, Asian
clear embossing ink & pen, gold embossing powder
gold pigment ink, heat tool
red paper: 2¼"x6", four 1" squares
Paper Pizazz™ patterned papers: white stripes on red,
    vellum, four 1⅜" squares of denim
2½"x6¼" blue cardstock
2" square gift box, 25" of ⅝" wide gold mesh ribbon, tape
metallic gold pen, tacky glue, ¼" hole punch, scissors, ruler

For the bookmark: Tear the vellum Paper Pizazz™
to 1¾"x5½". Draw around the edges with the
embossing pen, sprinkle with powder and emboss
(see page 28). Stamp and emboss three Primitive
images down the vellum Paper Pizazz™ center.
Randomly stamp gold Primitive images on the red
strip front. Use the gold pen to draw groups of three
dots on the vellum front. Round the corners of the
red strip and glue it to the blue cardstock. Lay the
vellum on th red strip, punch a hole through all
layers and tie a 9" length of ribbon to secure.

For the box: Stamp and emboss an Asian image on
each red square. Trim with patterned scissors and
glue to each denim Paper Pizazz™ center. Wrap the
box with the white stripes on red Paper Pizazz™ and
tape to secure. Glue a stamp image to each box side
and tie the remaining ribbon around the box in a
shoestring bow with 1" loops and 2" tails.

Decorative Foam Stamps

This chapter focuses on decorative foam stamps. They have broad surface foam images mounted on foam handles. The foam is what makes them so versatile to use.

These inexpensive foam stamps are very economical to manufacture so decorative foam stamp images are generally larger than wood handled images (though they come in all sizes). The doll bed and quilt project on page 132 shows how easily a strong focal point can be established with a decorative foam stamp, while the bug bags on page 134 prove you don't have to make a big project with these big stamps. On the other hand, the dress up hat box and box and album projects on page 133 show the great looks that can be created using some of the smaller foam images that are available.

Because of the foam that makes up these stamps, they bend easily making it possible to stamp rough or curved surfaces such as the bisque plates and mug on page 137 or the flower pot on page 139.

Decorative foam stamps were designed to be used with stamping paints. The non-absorbent foam makes them easy to clean. Stamping paint is designed to easily cover any surface, so these two products work well to stamp images onto anything including canvas floor-cloths (see page 136), unfinished wood (like the trout rack on page 139), painted wood (as was done over the sea sponged background on the country decorative plates on page 137) and, of course, all types of paper products from cardboard (like the toy box on page 134) to papier mâché (such as the hat box shown on page 133). Of course, they can also be used with inks. The projects on page 135 show how effective these large, broad surfaced images can be when stamped with embossing ink and embossed!

This chapter's background paper is from Paper Pizazz™ Handmade Papers.

Doll Bed & Bedding

Decorative stamps: Anemones,
  Accent Leaf
stamping paints: light green, dark
  green, purple, red, yellow
acrylic paints: white, lavender, yellow
14"x21" unfinished wood doll bed with
  head and footboards
¼ yard of white fabric
1 yard of green with pink flowers
  fabric
⅔ yard of purple with white, blue and
  red flowers fabric
½ yard each of white fabric and laven-
  der with white and pink
  flowers fabric
quilt batting: 12"x18", 18"x18"
paintbrushes: 1" wide flat, ¼" wide flat
3 oz. of fiberfill, thread, ruler
access to a sewing machine
scissors, straight pins, acrylic sealer
masking tape, sandpaper, soft cloth,
  new pencil with eraser

For the bed: Prepare the wood (see page 36). Paint the bed white and the knobs lavender, let dry. Use masking tape to mask off a 5" square on the head and footboard centers as shown. Paint the squares lavender and let dry. Mask off a ¼" wide strip around the lavender square and paint acrylic yellow, let dry. Blend (see page 27) purple and red stamping paints on the Anemones stamp and imprint the flowers as shown. Let dry. Repeat using light and dark green paints for the Leaves. Paint the flower centers yellow. Dip the pencil eraser into the yellow paint and touch it to the bed knobs for dots as shown. Let dry. Seal.

For the quilt: Refer to page 38 for stamping on fabric before beginning. Cut five 5" white fabric squares. Repeating the steps for stamping the head and footboard squares of the bed, stamp Anemones and Leaves in each fabric square center. Let dry. Cut four 5" lavender squares. Place a stamped and lavender square right sides together and sew one edge of the squares together. Open the squares and repeat by sewing another white stamped square to the opposite side of the lavender square. Repeat with the other squares alternating as shown to make a

total of 3 strips. Sew the long edges of the 3 strips together, making sure to line up the quilt blocks.

For the quilt binding: With right sides together, sew a 2½"x15" strip to each short edge of the quilt blocks. Sew a 2½"x18½" strip to the remaining two edges. Cut an 18"x18" green fabric piece. Place it and the quilt blocks right sides together and place an 18" square of batting on one side. Pin in place and sew 3 sides together. Turn right side out. Turn the raw edges under and sew the opening closed.

For the mattress: Cut a 12"x18" piece of purple fabric and a 12"x18" piece of green fabric. Place right sides together with a 12"x18" piece of batting on one side and pin the outer edges to secure. Sew around 3 sides and turn right side out. Turn the raw edges under and sew the opening closed.

For the pillow: Cut a 9"x5½" piece each of green fabric and lavender fabric. Place right sides together and sew 3 sides. Turn right side out and stuff with fiberfill. Turn the raw edges under and sew the opening closed.

Keepsake Box & Album

Cut Paper Peach
*   Decorative stamp*
acrylic paints: lavender,
*   ivory, teal, pink*
10"x12" unfinished wood
*   post-bound album*
6¾"x4½" unfinished wood
*   triangle box*
three 1½" wide round wood
*   knobs*
paintbrushes: 1" wide flat,
*   ¼" wide flat*
foam sponges, tacky glue
¾" wide masking tape
acrylic sealer, soft cloth,
*   sandpaper, screwdriver*

Disassemble the album. Prepare the wood pieces (see page 36). Paint the knobs, album bindings and box lid sides teal. Let dry. Place tape strips ¼" apart on the bindings and lid sides and paint ivory between them. Remove the tape and let dry.

Open the box and paint the box, lid top and both album cover pieces lavender. Let dry. Apply pink and teal paint to the stamp and randomly stamp the images to cover the lavender painted wood. Let dry. Use a brush to paint the peach centers ivory. Let dry. Seal all wood pieces. Glue the knobs to the bottom box corners as shown. Reassemble the album.

Dress Up Hat Box

Decorative stamps: Hat, Purse, Shoes
stamping paints, black, white, fuchsia, teal, purple, yellow
11½"x5¼" papier mâché hat box
2" wide round wood knob, 30" of 10 mm wide black cording
paintbrushes: ¼" wide flat, 1" wide flat
*   new pencil with eraser, ¾" wide masking tape*
*   two ¾" wide grommets & tool*
*   screw driver, 1" long screw, tacky glue, water-based sealer*

Seal the box. Paint the box white, the lid top fuchsia and the lid sides black. Let dry. Place many 5" long tape strips ¼" apart all the way around the box bottom. Paint yellow between the tape, remove the tape and let dry. Dip the eraser in white paint and touch it to the lid sides for dots as shown. Apply paints to the stamps and stamp them onto the box and lid as shown. Paint the knob black, let dry and use the eraser to make white dots as on the lid sides. Let dry then screw the screw through the inside lid center and into the knob hole filled with glue. Follow the grommet tool manufacturer's directions to insert the grommets into the box. Push one cording end through and tie a knot inside to secure. Repeat for the other side.

Bug Bags

Decorative stamps: Bee, Ladybug,
  Checkerboard
stamping paints: black, yellow, red
gift bags: yellow, white
5¼" square white card, yellow paper
white sticker paper
tissue paper: red checks, red dots,
  black dots
cardboard, scissors, tacky glue
Post-it® notes

For the Ladybug bag: Keep the bag
folded and insert a piece of cardboard.
Apply red and black paint to the stamp
and randomly stamp the Ladybug image
onto the bag front. Let dry. Remove the
cardboard, open the bag and insert the
dotted tissue papers.

For the Ladybug card: Use black paint to
stamp one row of the Checkerboard image around
the card edges as shown. Stamp a red and black
Ladybug on the goldenrod paper. Cut it to a 4¼" square
and glue it to the card center.

For the Bee bag: Keep the bag folded and insert a piece of
cardboard. Apply yellow and black paints to the stamp and
stamp two Bee images on sticker paper. Cut each out. Mask (see page 29) the outer ⅜" of the bag
front and paint the center bag black. Let it dry, remove the masks and mask the center. Use red
paint to stamp one row of the Checkerboard image around the border. Adhere the Bee images as
shown in the black area. Open the bag and insert the checked tissue paper.

Traveling Toy Box

Decorative stamps: Train Engine, Car, Airplane,
  Checkerboard, Alphabet
stamping paints: red, blue, yellow
13¾"x4¾"x10½" cardboard box with handle
foam sponges, masking tape, Post-it® notes
¼" wide flat paintbrush

Before beginning, stand the box up as shown and
orient the top, front and sides as related here. This
way, when the box is carried, the letters and
images are right side up. Use the masking tape to
tape off an 8"x6" rectangle on the box lid center.
Paint it yellow, remove the tape and let dry. Tape
off a ¼" border around it and paint it red. Remove
the tape and let dry. Use the letters to stamp the
child's name and "TRAVELING TOYS" as shown.
Use the Post-it® notes to mask (see page 29) the
rectangle. Apply paints to the appropriate portion of
each stamp and stamp the images onto the box lid as shown. Paint
the box side edges red. Stamp red Checkerboards on the top and bottom
box. Stamp blue Checkerboards on the box sides. Let dry.

Embossed Metal Box

Decorative stamps: Wrought Iron Tile, Wrought Iron Corner
clear embossing ink, gold embossing powder, heat tool
7" square papier mâché box
4⅜" square of copper metal sheeting
acrylic paints: brick, metallic gold
1" wide flat paintbrush
black with gold stripes handmade paper
foam sponges, 20 brass decorative upholstery tacks
deckle patterned scissors, straight edged scissors
tacky glue, long tongs, water-based sealer
paper towels, wire cutters, pencil

Seal the entire box. Paint the entire box brick and let dry. Dip the brush in gold paint then blot on paper towels until the brush is almost dry. Brush gold streaks over the brick paint. Let dry. Stamp and emboss (see page 28) the Corner stamp on the box sides. Stamp the Tile image onto the metal sheeting, hold with the tongs and emboss it. Let it cool then trim the edges with patterned scissors. Trace the box lid onto the handmade paper and cut out. Glue to the box lid top. Glue the sheeting to the box lid center as shown. Place a dab of glue under each tack head and press 5 tacks evenly spaced into each box lid side as shown. Let dry. Use the wire cutters to trim the ends of them inside the box lid.

Metallic Swirl Frame

Swirly Lines Decorative stamp
clear embossing ink, gold and copper embossing
  powders, heat tool
copper metal sheeting
11"x12½" unfinished wood frame with a
  4½"x6½" opening
black acrylic paint, water-based sealer
soft cloth, sandpaper, long tongs, scissors, tacky glue
masking tape, photograph

Prepare the wood (see page 36). Seal the frame, let it dry and paint it black. Let it dry. Stamp and emboss (see page 28) a partial copper image in each frame corner as shown. Stamp and emboss a partial gold image on each opening side as shown. Stamp two images onto the metal sheeting, sprinkle with gold powder, hold with the tongs and emboss. Let it cool and cut the center portion of each image to 4¼"x3". Seal the frame then glue the sheeting pieces above and below the frame opening. Tape the photo to show through the frame opening.

Sunflower Gift wrap

Decorative stamps: Sunflower, Leaves, Checkerboard
stamping paints: yellow, green, burnt orange, blue
kraft paper, black paper
gift box, black raffia
deckle patterned scissors, straight edged scissors, tape

Cut enough kraft paper to wrap the gift box. Randomly stamp yellow and burnt orange Sunflowers to cover the paper. Stamp green Leaves among the Sunflowers. Let dry. Wrap the gift box and tape to secure. Cut enough kraft and black papers to wrap around the width of the box. Stamp blue Checkerboards along the kraft paper. Use patterned scissors to cut the black length of paper to 3¼" wide and the kraft to 2¼" wide. Wrap the strips around the box as shown and tape each to secure. Tie the raffia around the Checkerboard paper ribbon strip into a shoestring bow (see page 41).

Country Heart Floorcloth

Decorative stamps: Plain Heart, Heart
in Hand, Open Heart
stamping paints: red, blue, green
30"x24" piece of floorcloth
acrylic paints: pink, ivory, brown,
mustard
1" wide flat paintbrush
¾" wide masking tape
ruler, new pencil with eraser

Paint the entire cloth ivory and let dry. Use the tape to mask a 1" wide border all the way around it. Paint the border blue, remove the tape and let dry. Beginning in the upper left corner and working clockwise, paint sections as follows: paint an 11"x9" brown section, skip a 4¼"x9" section leaving it ivory, paint a 12½"x9" pink section, paint an 11"x4¾" brown section, skip an 11"x8" section leaving it ivory, paint a 5"x12¾" mustard section, skip a 12"x8" section leaving it ivory, and paint a 12"x4¾" pink section. Let the cloth dry. To paint the upper left plaid section, paint five 1" wide vertical ivory stripes and four 1" wide horizontal ivory stripes evenly spaced. Repeat using mustard paint in the lower right section. Let dry. Apply tape strips lengthwise ⅛" apart in the pink upper right section. Paint ivory between the strips. Remove the tape and let dry. Apply paint to the appropriate portion of each stamp and stamp the images as shown in each section.

To finish the upper center ivory section, dip the pencil eraser in red paint and touch it by each heart tip as shown, then paint blue accent marks. To finish the right side brown section, paint blue dash lines around and among the hearts as shown. To finish the left side pink section, dip the pencil eraser in blue paint and touch it below each heart point, then paint green accent marks as shown. To finish the lower left ivory and lower center mustard sections, use the pencil eraser to make groups of three brown and individual ivory dots, respectively, as shown.

Floral Dishes

Decorative stamps: Rose, Checkerboard
bisqueware glazes: blue, pink, yellow, green
bisqueware pieces: one 10" plate, two 8" plates, one 2½" tall mug
foam sponges, paintbrushes: ¼" wide flat, ½" wide flat, #2 liner
soft cloth, ruler, access to a kiln

Prepare the bisqueware pieces (see page 37). After stamping, use the liner brush to re-apply glaze colors to deepen the hues as desired. After painting each piece, take them to a professional and have the pieces fired in a kiln.

For the top plate: Apply glaze to the appropriate portion of the Rose and stamp two of each color around the plate rim as shown. Use the paintbrush to paint green glaze stripes 1" apart to create the plaid pattern. Let dry. Paint pink glaze lines on the inside left and bottom sides of each resulting square. Let dry.

For the Checkerboard plate: Apply blue glaze to the Checkerboard image and stamp it around the plate rim. Stamp a yellow and green glaze rose in the plate center. Paint the surrounding plate center pink with a wavy yellow border as shown and let dry.

For the left plate: Paint pink glaze lines 1" apart along the plate rim to make the plaid as shown. Let dry. Paint yellow glaze lines on the left and bottom sides of the resulting squares. Paint a green glaze border around the plate center. Isolate (see page 29) the rose blossom of the image and stamp three yellow glaze images. Repeat for the green leaves as shown. Let dry.

For the mug: Use the ½" wide flat paintbrush to apply blue glaze strips ½" apart around the rim and handle as shown. Isolate the rose blossom portion and stamp three images evenly spaced around the cup. Let dry and repeat for the leaves as shown. Paint yellow glaze around the images. Let dry.

Country Decorative Plates

Decorative stamps: Rooster, Pig, Checkerboard
stamping paints: pink, red, orange, yellow, blue
acrylic paints: black, ivory
two 11½" wide unfinished wood plates
sea sponges, foam sponges, black medium-tip pen
½" wide paintbrush, soft cloth, toothbrush
sandpaper, water-based sealer

Prepare the wood (see page 36). Paint each plate ivory and let dry. Stamp blue Checkerboards onto each plate rim and let dry. Use the sea sponge to sponge blue paint onto the centers. Stamp a pink Pig in one plate center and paint the inner rim edge pink. Use the pen to write "le cochin" ("the pig") around the plate center. To spatter the plate, dampen the toothbrush and dip it into black paint then pull your thumb across the bristles. Let dry and seal. Repeat for the Rooster plate using the colors shown, but write "le coq" ("the rooster"), instead.

Olive Branch Footstool

Decorative stamps: Olive Branch, Checkerboard
stamping paints: olive green, ivory, black, yellow
19"x11½x"9" unfinished wood footstool
1" wide paintbrush, foam sponges
masking tape, water-based sealer
soft cloth, sandpaper

Prepare the wood (see page 36). Paint the center support yellow, the stool edges ivory and the remaining stool olive green. Let dry. Use the masking tape to tape off a 10½"x4⅝" rectangle on the stool top. Paint it yellow. Let dry. Apply paint to the appropriate portions of the Olive Branch stamp and stamp an image in the rectangle center. Let dry and mask (see page 29) it using tape. Mask a ½" border around the yellow rectangle and paint this ivory (you may need to apply two coats to cover the green). Let it dry. Apply black paint to the top row of the Checkerboard stamp. Stamp the isolated row in the ivory border. Repeat to stamp rows of black checks on all ivory areas. Let dry. Mask the stool top edges and center rectangle, apply yellow paint to the top portion of the Olive Branch stamp and randomly stamp the image on the stool top. Repeat using olive green and black paint to stamp the center support.

Olive Branch Welcome Sign

Decorative stamps: Olive Branch, Checkerboard
Uppercase Alphabet Stamp Set
stamping paints: ivory, olive green, black
12"x20" unfinished wood sign
1" wide flat paintbrush
foam sponges, toothbrush
water-based sealer, soft cloth, sandpaper

Prepare the wood (see page 36). Paint the top and bottom sign olive green. Paint the center ivory. Let dry. Stamp black Checkerboard images to cover the olive green paint. Let dry. Apply black and olive green paint to the appropriate portions of the Olive Branch stamp and impress five images to form a circle as shown in the sign center. Let dry. Stamp black letters to read "WELCOME FRIENDS" above and below the Olive Branch circle as shown. To spatter the sign with paint, dip the dampened toothbrush into black paint then pull your thumb across the bristles. Let dry and seal.

Trout Peg Rack

Trout Decorative stamp
pale ivory acrylic paint
19"x8" unfinished wood rack with 3 pegs
colored oil pencils: green, blue, black, orange, yellow, white, red, brown
metal ruler, old cloth, pencil, tacky glue, tracing paper
matte-finish wood sealer, oak wood stain, light wood stain
sandpaper, soft cloth, woodburning tool, heavy gloves

Remove the pegs. Prepare the wood pieces (see page 36). Use the pencil to lightly draw a border to follow the lines of the rack 1" in from the edge. Use the ruler and pencil to divide the border into 1" sections. Draw a double line divider (2 lines 1/8" apart instead of only 1 line) for every other section as shown. Apply pale ivory paint to the Trout stamp and stamp three fish inside the border as shown. Follow the manufacturer's directions to use the woodburning tool and go over the Trout outlines and detail lines, plus each drawn border line. Wear heavy gloves and use a metal ruler as a guide (which will get hot!) to help burn perfectly straight lines. Color the trout with oil pencils as shown. Color one border block green, one blue and the 1/8" strip between the double line dividers brown. Trace the fly patterns above and cut them out. Draw them onto the rack and go over the lines with the woodburning tool. Burn wavy lines for fishing line. Stain and seal the rack, let dry and seal again. Place the pegs into the holes filled with glue.

Ivy Flower Pot

Ivy Decorative stamp
acrylic paints: ivory, green, yellow, black
6½" wide terra cotta pot
1" wide paintbrush
foam sponges, sea sponges, acrylic sealer

Seal the pot and let dry. Paint the outside of the pot ivory, paint the pot rim green and let dry. Stamp green and yellow Ivy images around the pot as shown. Dip the sea sponge in black paint and sponge the pot rim black. Let dry. Use a plastic liner in the pot if you intend to grow a plant in it.

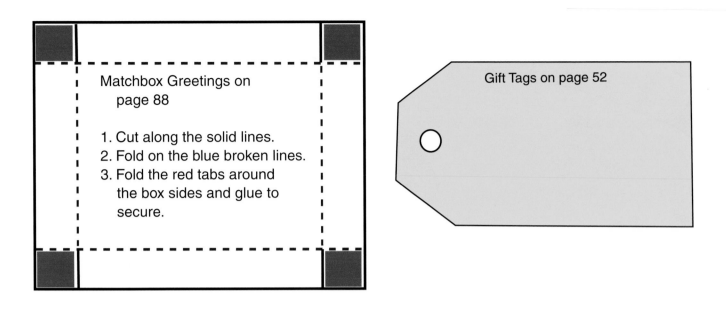

Matchbox Greetings on
page 88

1. Cut along the solid lines.
2. Fold on the blue broken lines.
3. Fold the red tabs around
   the box sides and glue to
   secure.

Gift Tags on page 52

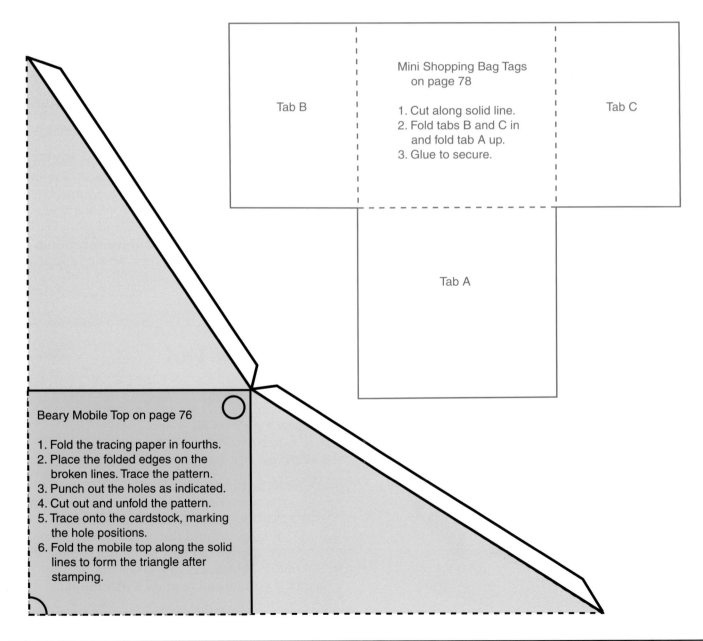

Mini Shopping Bag Tags
on page 78

1. Cut along solid line.
2. Fold tabs B and C in
   and fold tab A up.
3. Glue to secure.

Tab B

Tab C

Tab A

Beary Mobile Top on page 76

1. Fold the tracing paper in fourths.
2. Place the folded edges on the
   broken lines. Trace the pattern.
3. Punch out the holes as indicated.
4. Cut out and unfold the pattern.
5. Trace onto the cardstock, marking
   the hole positions.
6. Fold the mobile top along the solid
   lines to form the triangle after
   stamping.

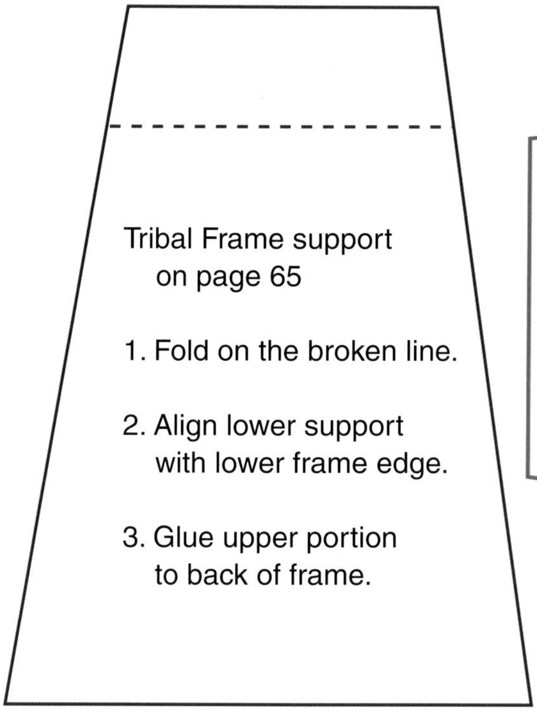

Tribal Frame support
on page 65

1. Fold on the broken line.

2. Align lower support
with lower frame edge.

3. Glue upper portion
to back of frame.

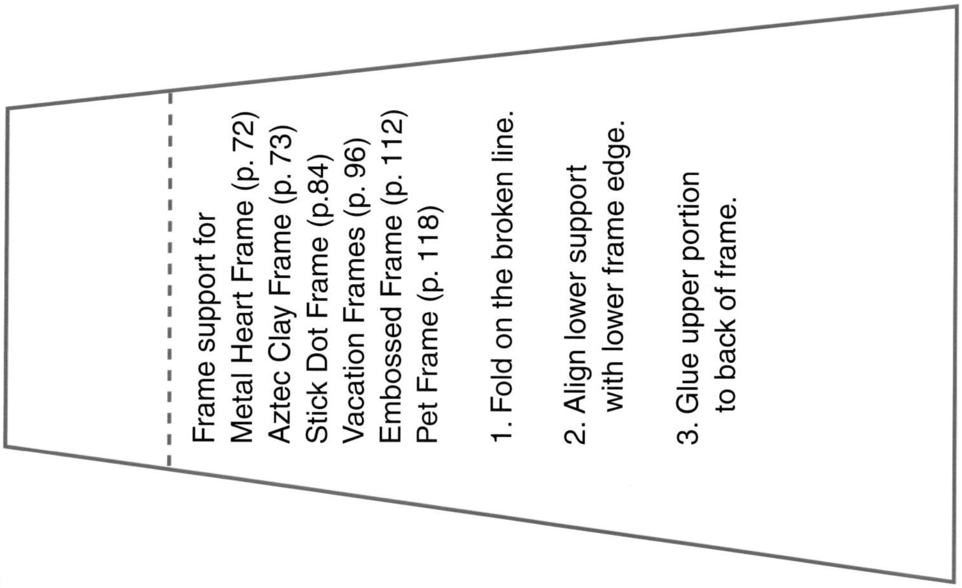

Frame support for
Metal Heart Frame (p. 72)
Aztec Clay Frame (p.73)
Stick Dot Frame (p.84)
Vacation Frames (p. 96)
Embossed Frame (p. 112)
Pet Frame (p. 118)

1. Fold on the broken line.

2. Align lower support
with lower frame edge.

3. Glue upper portion
to back of frame.

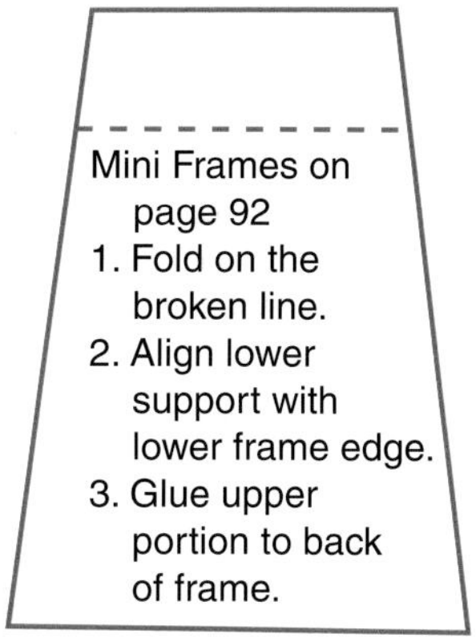

Mini Frames on
page 92
1. Fold on the
broken line.
2. Align lower
support with
lower frame edge.
3. Glue upper
portion to back
of frame.

Cloud pattern for Sponging on page 33

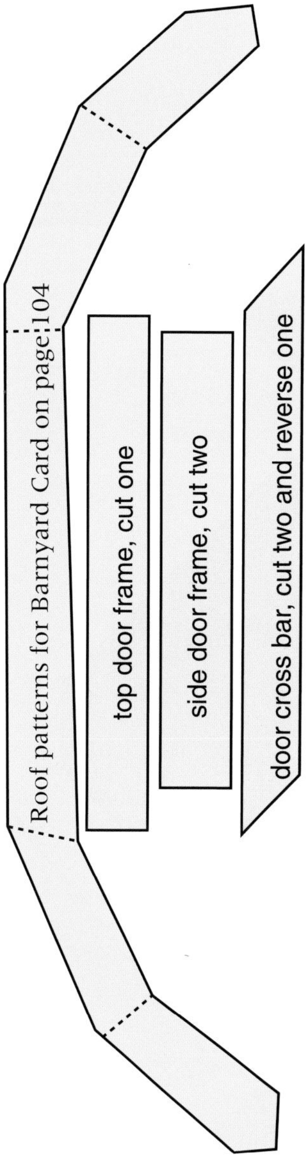

Roof patterns for Barnyard Card on page 104

top door frame, cut one

side door frame, cut two

door cross bar, cut two and reverse one

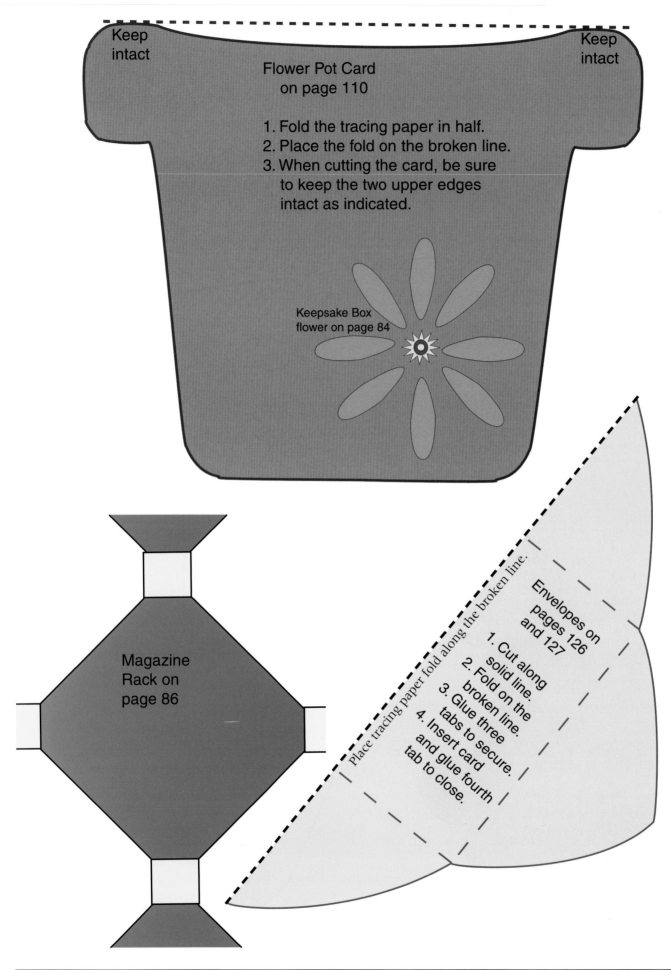

Keep
intact

Keep
intact

Flower Pot Card
on page 110

1. Fold the tracing paper in half.
2. Place the fold on the broken line.
3. When cutting the card, be sure
   to keep the two upper edges
   intact as indicated.

Keepsake Box
flower on page 84

Magazine
Rack on
page 86

Place tracing paper fold along the broken line.

Envelopes on
pages 126
and 127

1. Cut along
   solid line.
2. Fold on the
   broken line.
3. Glue three
   tabs to secure.
4. Insert card
   and glue fourth
   tab to close.

GLOSSARY

Air–dry modeling clay…modeling compound that holds its shape and air dries. Accepts most kinds of paints and inks well.

Brayer…a handled tool featuring a 4" wide rubber roller that is ideal for rolling wide bands of ink onto a surface.

Brush marker…a pen, usually with two tips of varying widths, filled with a multi-purpose ink. Available in many colors.

Cards In Minutes™…cards featuring patterns in a wide variety of themes and designs. Blank inside and suitable for a multitude of paper crafts. Available from Hot Off The Press.

Coated paper…paper that has a gloss or sheen to it. This paper has little or no absorbancy.

Collage…the art of layering and combining paper pieces and charms or other objects onto a surface.

Crafter's ink…a versatile ink suitable for stamping on a wide range of surfaces including fabric. Also called fabric ink.

Decorative foam stamp…a die cut shape, image or design cut from a dense foam sheet and adhered to a pliable foam handle.

Decoupage glue…a thin, liquid that adheres paper pieces to a surface. It dries clear, leaving a durable surface and may be used as a sealer. Not water submersible.

Emboss…to combine embossing ink and embossing powder with heat to create a raised, lustrous image. Inks and powders are available in clear or in a variety of colors.

Glaze…a colored or clear gel-like substance that produces a glossy, durable surface on ceramic or bisque pieces when properly cured.

Image…a stamped design.

Paper Pizazz™…acid-free, lignin-free sheets of paper featuring solid colors or patterns in a wide variety of themes and designs. Suitable for a multitude of paper crafts. Available from Hot Off The Press.

Pearl-EX…embossing powder of various particle size which creates a variety of looks from a smooth luster to a metallic sheen.

Polymer clay…a soft, moldable clay that becomes a hard plastic when baked in an oven.

Rubber stamp…a die cut shape, image or design cut from a rubber sheet and adhered to either a wood or foam handle.

Stamping paint…specially formulated paint which has an extended "open" drying time.

Textile marker…a pen, usually with two tips of varying widths, filled with a specially formulated ink suitable for most fabrics. Available in many colors.

Uncoated paper…paper that has no absorbancy-blocking sheen added. This paper varies in degrees of absorbancy.

Water-based sealer…a spray or liquid substance that produces a clear, durable surface. It is ideal for use as a base or final coat on wood projects.

Manufacturers & Suppliers

Delta Technical Coatings, Inc.
…for acrylic paints and foiling products
2550 Pellissier Place
Whittier, CA 90601
(213) 686-0678
www.deltacrafts.com

Dufeck Wood Products
…for unfinished wood pieces
P.O. Box 428
Denmark, WI 54208
(920) 863-2354

Highsmith Inc.
…for cardboard pieces
P.O. Box 800
Ft. Atkinson, WI 53538
(920) 563-9571

Hot Off The Press
…for patterned Paper Pizazz™ and patterned Cards In Minutes™
1250 N.W. Third St.
Canby, OR 97013
(503) 266-9102
www.paperpizazz.com

Jacquard Products
…for Pearl-EX embossing powder
1147 Healdsburg Ave.
Healdsburg, CA 95448
(707) 433-9577
www.jacquardproducts.com

Kolo
…for paper photo albums
241 Asylum St.
Hartford, CT 06103
(860) 547-0367
www.kolo-usa.com

Kunin Felt
…for floor cloth
380 Lafayette Rd.
Hampton, NH 03843
(603) 929-6100
www.kuninfelt.com

The Leather Factory
…for leather products
P.O. Box 50429
Fort Worth, TX 76105
(817) 496-4414
www.leatherfactory.com

Mixed Nuts
…for corrugated frames
221 Rayon Drive
Old Hickory, TN 37138
(615) 847-8399
www.kraftables.com

Polyform Products Co.
…for polymer clay
1901 Estes Ave.
Elk Grove Village, IL 60007
(847) 427-0020
www.sculpey.com

Rubber Stampede, Inc.
…for rubber and decorative stamps
P.O. Box 246
Berkeley, CA 94701
(800) NEAT-FUN (632-8386)
www.rstampede.com

Tsukineko Inc.
…for Pigment Dauber Duos
15411 N.E. 95th St.
Redmond, WA 98052
(425) 883-7733
www.tsukineko.com

Walnut Hollow
…for unfinished wood pieces
1409 State Road 23
Dodgeville, WI 53533
(608) 935-2341
www.walnuthollow.com